Alma Overholt, Santa Catalina Island

AVALON BAY

Veiled Horizons

stories of big game fish of the sea

Ralph Bandini

THE DERRYDALE PRESS
Lanham and New York

THE DERRYDALE PRESS

Published in the United States of America
by The Derrydale Press
4720 Boston Way, Lanham, Maryland 20706

ISBN 1-56416-199-4 (leatherbound : alk. paper)
ISBN 1-58667-076-X (pbk. : alk. paper)
Library of Congress Card Number: 2001086305

⊖™ The paper used in this publication meets the minimum requirements of
American National Standard for Information Sciences—Permanence of
Paper for Printed Library Materials, ANSI/NISO Z39.48–1992.
Manufactured in the United States of America.

TABLE OF CONTENTS

LIST OF ILLUSTRATIONS

VEILED HORIZONS

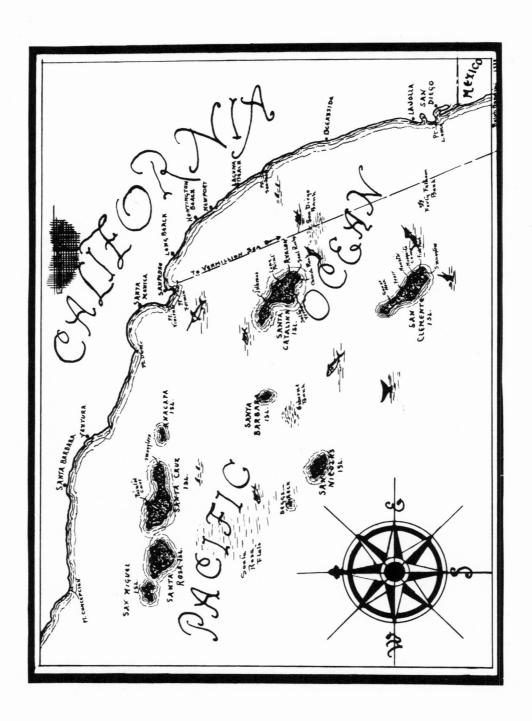

THE LAST FISH

IT is strange, as line spins off the reel of life, how various incidents and scenes that one has experienced over the years seem to weave and shuttle in a sort of kaleidoscope until, scarcely before one realizes that it has happened, they fall into their appointed places to form the crazy-quilt pattern which comprises the story of one's life. And it is strange, too, how the seemingly great things become small and the small things great. Rudyard Kipling knew what he was talking about when he wrote, "And that is why the big things pass, and the little things remain."

A good many years ago, on a sunny September morning, I came into Avalon Bay from San Clemente with the blue and white swordfish flag flying at the masthead. Upon the stern was lashed a 244-pound marlin, my first button fish. Since then I have gone through many experiences of vastly greater importance than that of bringing in a dead fish. Nevertheless the fact remains that, despite what I have done or shouldn't have done, accomplished or failed to accomplish, during the interim of those years, that morning remains startlingly clear in the album of memories. There was the official weighing-in—the congratulations of my fellow Club members—the putting into my lapel buttonhole of the coveted Tuna Club gold swordfish button by Tom Manning, then secretary—and the subsequent gathering of congenial souls in the Bait Box.

Of course there is a reason why that particular memory should remain so fresh after all those years between. Since my childhood we had always gone to Catalina Island for the summer. Before there was a Tuna Club, even before any man had been daring enough to attempt the taking of those great fish on rod and reel, I had watched the Italian fishermen, pulling homeward from their night's work, standing up at the oars, swinging rhythmically back and forth to the tempo of their native boat songs. Mornings without number my mother and I had gone out upon the bay in a skiff, had even ventured the three miles down to Seal Rocks, to catch yellowtail and bass on handlines. I shall never forget my first yellowtail taken on rod and reel—about a $3 outfit. I hooked him off Pebbly Beach Point—and it took me an hour and a half to land him! From those very earliest days, fishing has been to me the sport of sports. I've played golf and tennis, hunted, ridden and sailed—but always fishing has remained tops.

Later, as a lad, I often stood round-eyed and envying as those sturdy old pioneers of the game came in with their impossible catches taken on still more impossible tackle. When I think of them, and what they did, it seems to me that we so-called anglers of the present day, with our big, sturdy reels, our friction drags, our crank stops, our heavy lines and almost unbreakable rods, should hang our heads in shame! How they did it, God only knows! Three-piece jointed rods of wood, crude reels, flying crank handles, leather thumbstalls their only drag, lines that broke at less than forty pounds. What a breed of men they were—Holder, Morehouse, Dickerson, Ryder, Barrett, Stearns, Schenck, MacMillan, Manning, Potter, Reed, Earlscliffe, Murphy, Hooper, Boschen, Conn and all the rest! Those men *made* big game fishing, and it is due to them that you, today, have the sport, and have the equipment that their pioneering, their bruised and broken hands and fingers, brought into being. Try *their* way some time. Go out with a forty-pound line, a three-piece rod, a free-handle reel, and tie into a hundred-pound tuna! May God grant that, when our numbers go up, and the time comes for us to join them on the Happy Fishing Banks, we may have the decency to tread softly, carrying our hats in our hands, and listen respectfully when they are moved to speak of their deeds.

But to get back. As a lad I watched the Tuna Club come into being. Diffidently I hovered as close to the groups of those great anglers as the proprieties permitted, listening as they spun their yarns of days out upon the blue sea, of hours of desperate struggle with the hard-fighting battlers from out the deep. I even suffered with them as they nursed their wounds upon the verandah of the old Hotel Metropole. God knows I've suffered since!

With the famous old boatmen, Jim Gardner, Tad Gray, Mexican Joe, Monty Foster, Chappie, Joe Adargo, Percy Neale, George Johnson, Harry Elms and the rest, there was a little greater intimacy. They were not above permitting an admiring boy to help pull their skiffs up on the beach, to carry to their stands oars and gear, to let him listen as they told their stories of fish and fishermen.

As I grew older, membership in the Tuna Club seemed to me to be the ultimate of all possible ambition. There every worth-while quality was to be found—sportsmanship, courage, romance, adventure, good fellowship. Since then there have been times when those early beliefs have been sadly shaken—but the roots remain.

After a time the way opened whereby I could become an Associate Member—a sort of betwixt-and-between estate hovering upon the outskirts of the circle of the elect—truly a dry crust to a starving man. What I wanted above all things was Active Membership and the right to wear the Tuna Club button—and to that end I went to work enthusiastically and expensively.

From the very beginning everything seemed to go wrong. I

[3]

missed finding fish. When I did find them, I missed getting into the schools. When I did get into them, I missed strikes. When I did get hooked on, I pulled the hook out or broke the line. Reels froze on me. When I went over to Catalina the fish disappeared. As soon as I left, they came back. And, when none of these things happened, and I did actually land a fish, he was inevitably below the qualifying weight. I began to think I was "the mos' unluck' man" that ever lived!

But the old proverb holds true. It's a long lane that has no turn. In due time the one I was following came to a turn—although I had to go all the way over to San Clemente to find it. And so, that September morning, I came into Avalon with my first button fish.

Thereafter came more years of fishing. Various other buttons and prizes were kind enough to tumble into my lap, or climb up into my lapel buttonhole. I had a lot of fun. I didn't catch so very many fish —or any very large ones. I was soundly beaten by a lot more than I caught. But that is as it should be. A good licking once in a while is good for the peace of one's soul. It jerks one back to where one realizes one's proper place in the scheme of things. Various experiences, some of them strange, came my way. I called at out-of-the-way nooks and corners. I ran across a lot of good fellows—and some who were not so good. I gained a wholesome respect for those gentlemen adventurers of the seven seas—tuna, marlin swordfish and broadbill swordfish. Fishing was my greatest joy and I expected to keep on with it as long as I was able to sit in a chair and hold a rod.

Then came the year 1932. Marlin showed up in August. There weren't many, but what there were, were big. Three-hundred-pounders were the rule—not the exception.

Now I had never taken a three-hundred-pound marlin and, of

course, was anxious to get into the charmed circle. Accordingly I slipped over to Avalon for a day or two of fishing. Things weren't going so well for any of us in that year—as doubtless you remember. For me they were going very badly. One, perhaps two, day's fishing was the most I could afford. But at Avalon I got a break. Andy Martin, then president of the Tuna Club, invited me to go out with him, as his guest, for three or four days.

The first two were empty. We saw a few fish, all big ones, but they were wary and utterly indifferent to the bait. Those few who did rush it were hard to hook. Usually they would pick it up, then drop it immediately. Oddly enough I had all the strikes. Our baits would be swimming side by side, exactly alike, and yet every blessed fish crossed Andy's line to slash at mine. We changed seats, even rods—but still they hit my bait, not his. That's the luck of fishing!

The third day we worked far off the East End, then slanted in toward Salto Verde Point. It was a beautiful day. Out of the southwest rolled long, lazy seas, dimpled by the freshening westerly. Haze softened the rugged outlines of Catalina to a gentle blur. Here and there on the horizon other little fishing boats lifted into view as they climbed the swells, then slid out of sight again.

At about eleven o'clock we sighted three sickle fins riding down the swells. The very first glimpse of them told us they belonged to very large fish. The sight of marlin tails riding across the seas has never lost its thrill for me. There is something ghostly, unreal, about them. One moment the sea is empty. The next instant those slender sickle fins are all around you. Another, and they are gone, as you rub your eyes and wonder if you really saw them. These were off to one side and paralleling us. We speeded up, headed them, then slanted across in front of them.

Straight toward our baits they came, weaving, twisting, rising high, then sinking until just the tips of them showed. There was a tense moment as they crossed where our baits were, or should have been—we couldn't see them—and then we both swore. They passed by and went serenely on their way. Of course we came about and took after them again, but with little hope in our hearts.

Suddenly, just as the boat swung, there was a swift shadow by my bait, a spreading swirl, the sound of ripping silk, a savage jerk—then the rattle and click of the reel.

Straight away for San Clemente he headed. There was no short run, then stop, as is usual with a marlin. For him a straight line was the shortest distance between two points. He knew where he wanted to go and set out to get there in the least possible time. All I could do was to set the drag and hope he would strike himself.

No sooner did he feel the weight of the drag than he tore out of the water as though shot from a cannon. Out he came, a shining, twisting bulk of fury. Three times he jumped, clearing the water by a good ten feet, and shooting straight through the air all of twenty-five feet. After the third leap the drag of the line—and there was a lot of it out—seemed to bother him. He threshed and wallowed for a minute or two, beating the air with his sword. Then out he came again. But this time he didn't leap. Instead, he reared his great body out at a sixty-degree angle, and started "walking on his tail." That stunt of a marlin is something to see! Out they come until their tail, and a foot of their body forward of it, is in the water. Then they start rushing ahead, the tail apparently giving them the propelling power. How they keep that body up at such a steep angle, and for so long a time, is beyond me—but they do it. This one put on the greatest show of tail-walking I ever saw.

[6]

Straight out to sea he roared, throwing white water twenty feet on either side. Andy yelled to his captain to swing after him. In making the turn I lost a lot of line. I was using my big Coxe reel with eighteen hundred feet of twenty-four. When we once got squared around and after him I shivered when I saw how little was left on the spindle.

I hope I can paint the picture for you. The blue Clemente Channel, Catalina off to starboard, just a vague mass in the haze, and ahead of us that writhing, twisting, silver creature, standing almost erect, and throwing water on either side like the bow wave of a speedboat as he raced seaward. I had seen a lot of things in fishing, but never the equal of that! There was no fighting that fish. If we merely hung on we would be lucky. The line ran so directly forward that I had to lean far out to prevent it from fouling the forward stays. The *Erna* was good for about fourteen knots. She was almost wide open and yet that fish continued to take line. It doesn't seem possible, but it's true. I hadn't the slightest hope of saving him. It could only be a matter of minutes before that line, with so much of it out, would break of its own weight. But, strangely enough, it didn't—just another instance of the terrific punishment a twenty-four will stand. Why do anglers insist on going after a big fish with lines that are the first cousins of a rope!

Flesh and blood and courage couldn't keep up such a run forever. Something had to give. This time that something was the fish. With one last, desperate lunge he smashed back and started racing around us in a big circle, and just below the surface. Of course that furious run had stopped, but we were far from being out of danger yet. Instead of being out on a straight pull the line now had a big bag in it. I pumped furiously, picking up as much slack as I could, until at last he gave up those tactics and plunged downward. Again twenty-four thread had stood an unbelievable test.

At first the lunge downward was fast and furious. Then, little by little, it slowed into a heavy, sullen sinking, precisely like a broadbill. Then it stopped—except for short, heavy surges.

There we were. I judged that there were about eight hundred feet out. I tightened up and went to work—but got nowhere at all. In fact I lost some more line. Those surges took it away in spite of everything I could do. Furthermore we weren't able to get away on an angle from him. A fish that sticks right under the boat is the hardest kind there is to fight.

I pumped and reeled and pumped and reeled—or rather I pumped without doing very much reeling. Sometimes I gained a few feet, but only to lose it again. I didn't like the looks of things. I didn't like those sullen, heavy surges—our pulling right back over the fish each time that we tried moving a little away from him—the dead weight of him. I had experienced such things before and knew what they meant. Andy was standing beside me and his face, too, was grave. Turning to him I said,

"Andy, this fish is dead down there. I haven't felt any live movement for fifteen minutes."

He nodded. "I think so, too," he replied, adding, "Well, there's nothing for it but to pump him up. Better go after him." He knew, having been in that same spot too.

Just to make sure, I tried surging on him. By that I mean tightening up solid on the drag and surging the rod up and down. That trick will usually start a stubborn fish into doing something or other. I might as well have surged against the ocean bottom! I grew worried after half an hour. I had worked very hard and was getting tired. And, despite everything I did, or tried to do, I still kept losing a little line. I asked Andy to take charge of the boat, knowing that I would need all the help there that I could get.

The next two hours were just plain hell. I said I was tired out—and I was! I was tied on to a big fish who was dead down there about eight hundred feet. In spite of my utmost effort he was steadily sinking further. It was getting rough as the daily westerly freshened. At times I thought I had him coming, then a big sea would throw us and I would lose all I had gained. My cousin, Johnnie Winston, came up in his *Frances Ann* and watched us for five or ten minutes. Later on, back in Avalon, and after it was all over, he told me he had never seen anybody work so hard on a fish.

"You were pulling yourself out of the chair every time you lifted on him!" he said.

Perhaps I was, but I was unconscious of it at the time. The only thing I could think of was to work that fish upward until he started planing. There was but one thing about it, such work couldn't be kept up forever. Something was bound to give—either the tackle, the fish, or I. It was the fish.

Little by little—only inch by inch, at first—then, later, foot by foot, and finally yards at a time—I gained line. It piled back, dark, ragged and irregular. Suddenly Andy yelled, "*Look out!*" Three big seas were rushing toward us. I thumbed the line and held on for dear life. They passed under us without my losing more than three or four feet. I started pumping up again. Just as I came up a cross sea caught us under the counter. I was nearly jerked from the chair. I felt something give inside me. There was a stab of sharp pain—then a dull ache. But I paid little attention to it. The fish was coming nicely and I had plenty to do to guard against accidents, and the bucking and kicking of the *Erna*, without worrying about a few aches and pains.

Wet line kept piling back on the reel in wet, dripping ridges. It was coming in with less effort on my part every minute. In fact it was more or less a question of picking it up. The fish was planing. But despite the easing of the hard gruelling work of pumping up a dead weight a strange sort of weariness seemed to weigh me down. During my years of fishing there had been numberless times when I had been very, very tired. There were numberless times when I had thought I was going to die—afraid I wouldn't—and didn't! But this strange feeling was different. It was as though the bottom had dropped out of things—as though I were two separate and distinct persons, one of whom struggled and strained to accomplish something while the other stood by and watched with a sort of what's-the-use attitude.

Faster and faster the fish rolled up to the surface. The line moved steadily away from the boat. Andy yelled and pointed off to port. There he was—an indistinct bulk of shifting purple, green, silver and gold, rolling log-like in the heavy swells. Very carefully we eased over toward him. The swivel came out. Andy reached and grabbed it. I glanced at my watch. Three hours and fifty-five minutes!

He *was* dead. Sullenly his big body rolled and thumped against the side of the boat. Not a fin quivered. There was no need of any gaff. All we had to do was to get a rope around his tail—although that was none too easy a job in such a heavy sea. Andy and I started to haul him on board. I say "Andy and I" advisedly. As a matter of fact I couldn't pull a pound. I remember vaguely wondering why. In the past I had been able to pull fish up to two hundred and fifty pounds on board without any help from anybody. But not this time.

THE LAST FISH

We got him aboard somehow, but with no thanks to any help of mine. Once laid across the stern we could see that while he was big enough he wasn't of any extraordinary size—close to three hundred, one way or the other. We examined him carefully to see what might have killed him. There was no evidence of his having been fouled in the leader. He was hooked in the bony part of the upper jaw and the hook had chewed a hole as big as one's finger. I don't know what kept it from falling out.

Andy and I made up our minds that but one thing could have happened. In his mad surface run, his headlong downward dive, he must have burst a blood vessel, or whatever is the equivalent in a fish. Down deep—down in the blue caverns which had been his home, his stout heart had failed him, and he had died. Not a bad place or way to go, at that.

All the way back to Avalon—that night—and for days and weeks afterward, I had that queer feeling of lassitude. Nothing seemed to matter. I didn't know it then, but *my* run had slowed and stopped—my line had come to its end. Before many weeks were passed, instead of being out on the wide blue sea I loved so well, I was stretched out upon operating tables and in hospital beds for months. The days of my fishing were gone forever. I had joined the little army of those whom big game fishing had wrecked—or killed.

Well, it's been well worth the price it demanded. In another book of fishing tales I remember writing that, as I found myself approaching the end of the trail and my fishing days over, I would sit in front of the fire at night and cast my lure into the Sea of Memories. The wind might moan under the eaves, the rain might beat against the windows—but I wouldn't hear it. Instead, I would be out upon the wide blue sea—my sea. I would feel the sting of wind and sun and salt in my face. I would see the milling, screaming sea birds, the stabbing splashes on far horizons, weaving, arrogant fins. When I wrote that I little knew how very near that time had come. And the strange part of it is that I never wrote truer words in all my life!

By the mercy of God I live by the sea, on Santa Monica Bay. It is a beautiful body of water, bluer than summer skies. To the north there are the blue mountains of the Malibu—to the south the brown hills of the Palos Verdes—to the west—far horizons. I sit at my window and see visions.

Faces of old friends who, over the years, have made the long traverse to the Happy Fishing Banks, peer through the glass at me and smile. I'm not so sure but that those smiles are a bit too friendly, too welcoming. But they seem to tell me that where *they* are the sea is always blue, sun and sky are gentle, and fish are big. That may be all very well, but they can have it for themselves for a while. Me, I am nowhere near ready to join them. Even if I can't fish I can at least think about the times when I could and did.

I see purple islands half veiled with haze, sweeps of yellow wild oats lifting to a golden sky. Down their coasts we ride the long purple seas. Our shimmering bait slips temptingly along astern of us. What's that? A flash of purple, a wavering shadow, the sound of ripping silk, a spreading swirl of green. *"Swordfish! Swordfish!"*

The sea is empty—a world of veiled horizons. Above us is a little patch of red, vivid against the blue. Off to starboard the flying fish skitters and jumps and splashes. There is a burst of smoking water. A bronze torpedo lunges out. White water throws. The snarl of the deep sea reel crescendoes into the scream of tortured metal. *"Tuna! Bluefin tuna!"*

Again the empty ocean, glassy smooth except for the lazy rollers, stretching away to the world's end. What's that—right over there —just off the port bow? There it is again! Two crescent fins weaving arrogantly across the restless, heaving waters. The bait is in front of him, sinking. He hesitates an instant, then flicks his big tail and goes down to it. A breathless moment or two and then there's a gentle tug. The slack line straightens and moves out and off to one side. The reel clicks faster and faster. We're hooked on! *"Broadbill! Broadbill!"*

And those are not all the pictures that shuttle across the face of my window, by any means. Lonely coves at night. The rumble and crumple and thump of surf on the reef. The mournful barking of sea lions. The shrill scolding of an awakened sea bird. The bleat of goats, the sharp bark of a fox from the cliffs overhead. Brick red islands rising out of a lonely sea. Strange, primitive folk. The dirge of wind through rigging. The never silent whisper of restless waters. The sun coming up through fog with a path of gold leading straight to it—and up that path, black in the morning light, a single swordfish—jumping. Sunsets, the sun, flattened and distorted, sinking red into a crimson sea. Purple twilight settling stealthily as the sea takes on all the mystery, all the immensity which comes to it with the falling of night. Little white fishing boats, lifting over the seas, dropping from sight, only to lift again, and then, at the day's end, scuttling homeward to the welcoming lights of Avalon Town.

I am not becoming sentimental. Nor am I sorry for myself. I have nothing to be sorry for. I have had a lot of fun. I am going to have a lot more. It is just this. I am trying to express what big game fishing has meant to me—what it has left me with when I have been throttled down to a dead slow bell. I wouldn't have missed it for anything in the world. It is a grand, grand game. It broadens one's horizons, straightens out one's focus, sweeps the cobwebs out of one's brain. When you reach what you think is the ultimate end of your rope, you will find that a little stretch has been provided—just a little something more that makes it possible for you to carry on, and on—and on. When the days of the game are ended for you, it leaves you something to fall back upon—memories. And you, too, can sit at *your* window and see visions until the clatter and clack of civilization fade into the restless murmur of lonely waters.

VEILED HORIZON OFF CATALINA ISLAND

VEILED HORIZONS

IT is strange how relatively unimportant things stick in one's memory. Now I suppose I have made a hundred and more trips from Catalina over to San Clemente Island. I like the place. Most people don't. If ever there was a barren, God-forsaken, wind-swept, lonely, desolate spot, San Clemente Island is it. Probably that is why I like it. I like the cold fog-wind howling across it at dusk. I like its sweeping slopes of golden wild oats slashed by forbidding canyons. I like the sand dunes marching across its westerly end to pour in a white flood over the dark cliffs of its northerly side and down into the sea. I like the blue surges that tramp down its coast in endless procession, here and there breaking in a smother of white upon some outlying reef or rock. I like the great Pacific rollers crashing against the jagged, black teeth of China Point, throwing baffled spray fifty feet into the air. I like breakers smashing upon the reef that runs out from Pyramid Head. I like to see them start to lift far out, gathering height and momentum as they rush shoreward; the sun-shot green of their crests as they start to curl; the turmoil of white and green water as the reef tears them to shreds. I like the criss-cross, zig-zag goat trails on the steep hillsides; the sight of a flock scrambling upward, a big, bearded patriarch leading, the wobbly-legged kids struggling desperately to keep up; to hear them bleating at night on the cliffs far above. Most of all, I think, I like the loneliness of the place; the absence of hustling, crowding fellow humans.

Yes, I have made a lot of trips over there, partly because I like it, and partly because there the fishing is good. But of all these trips there is one that to this day stands out in my memory from all the rest—and I don't know why. There was nothing unusual about it. The fishing wasn't anything out of the ordinary. It happened over twenty years ago. But it still sticks with me—and I think it always will.

We pulled out from Avalon just before sunrise. It was as we rounded Seal Rocks at the East End that the sun broke through a fog bank and turned the sea from grey to rose to gold. Big lazy surges, hinting at illimitable wastes, rolled in from the southwest.

There was no life in sight but one solitary grouper fisherman about a mile and a half off the point, lifting into sight and disappearing as the seas rolled up under him and then dropped him into the valleys between, an occasional questing sea bird, and the sleek brown shapes of the sea lions basking upon the rocks.

I climbed on top the cabin and promptly set to work dreaming daydreams—a habit I have that seriously interferes with my fishing!

As we climbed to the crest of a big roller it was as though the whole wide world, and all its peoples, came into the range of our vision. Westward, vague and shadowy, appeared clumsy, square-sailed junks, beating their way against the flood of turbid, yellow rivers amid the clamor of gongs and the scream of conches. The murmur of the sea against the hull metamorphosed into the slip-slop and shuffle of myriads of sandalled feet. Was that sudden noise the squeak of a tortured fiddle, or only a sea bird scolding? Was that almost imperceptible odor the smell of the East, or only the breath of the sea?

That sullen mutter rumbling up out of the southwest—was it just the voices of the waters, or the rumble and thud of cannibal drums, the thunder of surf upon lonely coral reefs, the cadence of savage chants? And again, was that odor the breath of the sea, or whiffs of fragrance from scented islands?

Anyhow, north and south and west, and all the points between, the world was there before us—"for to see and for to admire."

"Ya better git goin'!" The parted curtain closed again and I came back abruptly to the job at hand. The voice was Roy's, my captain. "Yeah, ya better git goin'." He deftly slipped a flying fish bait on the hook and let out two others aptly called teasers.

"There's more swordfish out 'n this here channel than I ever seen," he went on. "An' that ain't all." Here he lowered his voice confidentially, hallmark of his craft, and glanced around furtively as though fearing he might be overheard. "Mike Marinkovitch told me last night he seen big yellowfin tunny over to Clemente. Swore they come up all 'round him when he wuz grouper fishin' over there! Mike ain't never lied to me yet—leastwise I ain't never caught him at it."

Then he took off his cap, scratched his head behind the ear, reached into his shirt pocket and pulled out and lit a very crumpled cigarette, and regarded me reflectively. At last he seemed to make up his mind to something.

"Lissen here," he said. "I know you. Ya bin settin' there thinkin' 'bout God knows what! Now ya can't catch no swordfish thinkin' 'bout anythin' but swordfish. An' ya can't catch 'em 'less ya fish for 'em. Nobody never caught nothin' yet with th' bait in th' bait box! Keep a bug draggin' all th' time, that's my motto." (A bug is Catalina parlance for flying fish.) "Now settle yerself down an' git yer mind on fishin'. Keep watchin' th' bait all th' time, an' them teasers, too. I'm goin' on top to keep watch 'round."

Well, that was that. God knows I have had the same sermon

preached me enough times! Obediently I settled back in the fishing chair, rod at alert, and watched the bait and "them teasers."

Sitting there, watching the bait, the teasers, and the long, lazy seas, my mind turned to Roy's little homily. The more I thought about it, the better I liked it. Whether he realized it or not, there was a heap of sound philosophy there. "Nobody never caught nothin' yet with th' bait in th' bait box." Damned true! Wasn't it Kipling who said, "Keep your light a-shining a little ahead of the rest"? And a long way further back than Kipling one of the old prophets mentioned something or other about not hiding one's light under a bushel. Sifted down to fundamentals they all meant the same thing, the ancient prophet, Rudyard Kipling and Roy. If you have a job to do, keep your mind on it and do it—and the very best you know how. Strange what one can learn from fishing!

"Bang! Jerk!" The rod almost jerked out of my hand. Line whizzed off with a whir and a click. A wide green swirl eddied and spread where the bait had been. I would have sworn I had never taken my eyes from it, and yet something had lashed up and grabbed it.

"Strike! Strike!" I shouted.

There was a thud behind me and Roy's disgusted voice.

"Damned bonito shark. Reel up!"

Sure enough, shark it was. Just the head of the flying fish was left and on it were those unmistakable teeth marks.

There he was, right under the stern—a sinister brown shape. Roy frantically hauled in the teasers, cursing softly. He literally jerked one out of the shark's very mouth and tossed them upon the stern deck, then regarded me darkly.

"Humph!" he grunted. "Didn't ya see that bird? How many

times I gotta tell ya to keep them eyes o' yourn peeled? Next time one o' them bastards shows up, reel like hell and holler fer me! We ain't got no bait to waste on them birds. Naw, don't let out for a piece. Wait till we git clean away from 'im."

Safely away from the thief, I let out the new bait. A big shear-water saw it. Cocking his head on one side, he hovered, eyed it, and decided that it was good. At the same time there was something about it that didn't look quite natural. He swooped and slid back and forth, twisting his head, making tentative little dives, then catching himself with banked wings. One could almost read what was going on in his mind. That shimmering thing down there looked like a fish and probably was a fish, but it didn't act like one. It looked easy enough to snap up—too easy! There must be a catch in it some place. Once he passed it up entirely and slid away to leeward. But recollection of that tempting morsel must have been too much for him. In a minute or two he was back again, and, tossing caution to the winds, plumped down upon it—or where it had been. Of course he missed it, and how shamefaced he appeared as he tentatively pecked at himself and shook his wings. For a moment or two he sat there, glancing around as though he were seeking to learn if anyone had seen him or not. Then he took off, only to come back in a minute or two and put on the same show over again.

Tiring of watching him and the bait, and "them teasers," and because we were well out in the channel now, in deep water where the chances of picking up a fish were slim, I lashed the rod to the chair and climbed on top the cabin beside Roy.

My welcome was none too cordial. He looked sidewise at me and grunted. Then, very pointedly, he looked back at the shimmering bait, the teasers, and back to me again. Shaking his head, he reached into his pocket for a cigarette, shielded the match with his hands, and lit it. His every expression, his every motion, told plainer than words that I had no business up there; that I should be down in the chair, holding the rod. But I didn't care what he thought—very much! I was my own master and could do as I pleased. If it suited my pleasure to sit on top the cabin and let the rod take care of itself, sit there I would. If, in so doing, we happened to miss a fish that again was my business—and my loss. So I settled myself comfortably and lit a cigarette on my own account.

The daily westerly had not yet come up, but its advance guard, in the form of vagrant puffs, was already ruffling the surface to a darker blue. A grey-blue sea, darkened here and there as wind riffled the surface; horizonless, as sea and sky were lost in the haze; and Catalina, its rugged outlines softened, dropping slowly astern. Shearwaters swept back and forth on their endless quest for food. How in the world do they contrive to brush the tops of the surges with their wing tips, and yet never hit! If we knew that trick we could really say we flew. Brown terns, white terns, terns that were black and white and brown and white, flapped along with that graceful, jerky motion that is so peculiarly their own. High up a gull beat steadily seaward, going somewhere and knowing where and why he was going. Off to starboard the water darkened with a queer jiggle, shot with silver. Birds wheeled abruptly to race down to it.

"Bait workin'," Roy observed, his first words since I had joined him on top.

Just beyond the bait the dark, triangular fin of a shark cut the surface. But he was too far away to trouble us.

I glanced backward. Catalina was but a dim mass. Within the hour it would have disappeared entirely and we would be alone upon the sea. There is something eerie about that. There one is, all alone, the center of a circle whose rim always remains the same distance away. For all one's eyes tell one there is nothing ahead but limitless wastes of restless, lonely waters. One might go on, and on, and on, and on, until, with a final gasp and gurgle, the engine died, and there one would remain until that fateful day when the sea shall give up her dead. Nice thought! I lit another cigarette, and thought of other things. As a matter of fact, ahead, in the haze, was San Clemente with its slopes of golden wild oats, its canyons, its friendly, sun-washed beaches, its dark cliffs bordered with the yellow of kelp and the cream of surf. In due time it would come out of the haze and we would be near our journey's end.

Catalina did disappear astern and for an hour we chugged steadily forward toward the fog that forever fled before us. Presently, however, there came a thickening of the mists ahead; a vague hint of something more substantial than haze. Then, with the rising wind, the fog was ripped to shreds and Clemente, lonely and sun-washed, lay before us.

"SWISSSSSH! CRAAAAAASSH! RRRRRRRRRRRR!"

We both tumbled off the cabin, Roy to the controls as he threw her into reverse and I to the rod where I fumbled frantically with the lashings.

"RRRRRRRRRRRRRRRRRRRRRRRRRRRRRRRRRRR!"

"Hit him!" Roy shouted.

I got the plagued thing free at last, jammed the butt into the seat socket, climbed over it somehow, and jerked hard. Far off to one side the water boiled and churned as a slender rapier beat the air. Then out he came.

"*Swordfish!*" we both yelled together.

Flick! Flick! Flick! Flick! Flick! Away he went in great, plunging leaps, so close together you couldn't count them. Line was whirling off the reel so fast it made me dizzy to look at it. There was a fearful lot of it out and he showed no sign of slowing. I think I turned Christian then and there. Never again would I leave a rod unattended. I wonder how many times I've sworn that very thing!

Somehow or other Roy had the boat turned and we were following him, but very slowly as the bag of the line steadily became bigger. He shook his head.

"Gotta pick up line faster'n that!" he barked.

That wasn't so easy to do. The weight of the line itself was hard to reel in. Furthermore the fish was still tearing along, in and out of the water, as though he would never stop. But if that bag was hard on me it was harder on him. The run slowed perceptibly. There was one last lunge, a sullen smash back, a moment of threshing on the surface, then he sounded. The voice of the reel deepened from its first high pitched scream to a throaty snarl.

He was plunging downward, but that first long run, dragging the heavy line, had tired him. Not being able to do anything with him yet I took the opportunity to get straightened around and flex out the first hand and muscle cramps that always come. Then I finished picking up whatever slack line was still more or less on the surface. I threw off my hat, peeled off my sweater, opened my collar, and got ready for whatever might be before us—half an hour— four or five hours. That's one thing about fishing. One never knows.

The downward lunge slowed and stopped. Roy threw out the clutch and we paid off broadside to the seas. He came aft, looked at the line left on the reel, at the angle where it entered the water, at the bending, stabbing rod.

"Better git after 'im!" he said, and went back to the controls.

Getting after him means that the fun has ended and the work begun. There is but one method of working a big fish up out of the depths. Pump and reel—pump and reel—pump and reel. Strain and heave until you lift your rod to an angle of about forty-five degrees, then drop quickly and pick up the slack. Be careful not to lift too high, or drop too low. Either threatens disaster. Sometimes you gain feet and yards, other times only inches. More often you lose instead of gaining. It is hard, hard work—make no mistake about that— and I for one have never found any way to make it easier. Arms, hands, fingers, legs, back—they all ache. Sweat pours into the eyes, half blinding you. Water drips off the line, down the rod, into your lap and thence to the floor where it forms a little puddle in which your feet slip and slither. There is never a moment's rest. If you let up on a fish for even a minute he will get his head on you and there is no telling how long you will be on him. Many is the angler who has learned that lesson through bitterness and pain! A big fish is stronger than you, he will recuperate faster than you can. Once you have him coming, you have to keep him coming—if you can. You have advantages: a boat skillfully maneuvered, reels with every labor-saving device, strong rods and lines. But to offset these the fish has strength and sheer, gallant courage. The odds are about even.

I tightened up the drag as much as I dared and went to work. For a few minutes we seemed to struggle, neither gaining any notice-able advantage, then, suddenly, he started up. I pumped furiously, trying to keep up with him, piling line back in wet, irregular ridges that dripped salt water into my lap and onto the deck. I wondered if he was going to be one of those few easy ones who make one furious run and are then all in.

No such luck. Suddenly the rod was almost torn from my grasp and back down he lunged, this time almost as fast as had been his surface run.

I groaned inwardly! Suppose he took it into his head to stay down there and sulk? That would spell hours of the hardest kind of work lifting him back up again.

We were in reverse, trying to ease the strain. Little waves slapped up against the stern. The reverse gear ground and churned.

The downward plunge slowed to little, short rushes, then stopped. I tightened up once more and went to work pumping and reeling. But I didn't get very far. Sometimes I gained a few feet, only to lose them again. The fish hung there, stubborn and sullen.

Then the strain eased. The line began to move away from us. He was surfacing again. I had to work hard to pick up the slack.

"CRAAAASSSSH!" There was a flurry of boiling water a few hundred feet to starboard and he lunged two-thirds of his length out, a furious thing of threshing sword, wagging head and great gaping jaws. Again he came out—clear this time, shooting through the air in a twisting arc. Once! Twice! Three times! Six! Seven! Ten! And a little while before I had thought he was all in!

But he *was* tired—that was manifest. The lunges were more sullen, sluggish; not the clean, twisting jumps of his first run. Presently even they subsided into heavy rolls and threshing of tail and sword. Then he started swimming slowly, just under the surface, half his dorsal fin showing, trying desperately to turn away from the boat but unable to conquer the weight of the drag and the arc of the bending rod. Now was the time to go after him—hard. And now, too, was one of the most dangerous points of the battle. He was on the surface about three hundred feet away. The line led almost straight to him.

Drop the rod a little too low, or if he turned his head suddenly on the uplift, the reward might very well be a broken line.

Working very carefully, watching the tip every second, I pumped him over, Roy aiding in working the boat closer. Never an inch did he give other than grudgingly. More than once he overcame the drag and tore off line. But he was deathly tired. Only his splendid, fighting spirit kept him twisting, turning, whirling about and reversing himself, wagging his great head and glaring at us with those big yellow eyes. And what a thing of beauty he was there in that clear, sun-shot water—a great dark shape of wavering greens, purples, silver and gold! The light distortion seemed but to intensify the brilliancy of those colors.

The swivel came out, hung a second—the line vibrating under the strain until little drops of water flicked off it, to form miniature rainbows—then jerked under again as he surged downward. Again it came out, hung, then, as I lifted, shot upward. I swung the tip forward. Roy reached out and grabbed the leader, quickly pulling the fish alongside, where he thumped and pounded, beating boat and water with sword and tail. Tired as he was, he was far from dead. We both stared at him. Roy looked at me questioningly.

He wasn't a large fish—probably not more than 175 pounds. We would be at Clemente for several days. Long before we were ready to return to Avalon he would be reeking carrion, unless there was some boat there that happened to be going back the next morning.

"Cut him loose!" I ordered.

Roy grinned and whipped out a pair of wire cutters. I think the rascal had had them in his hand all the time. Gently he lifted the great head. The hook was caught in the upper jaw, just inside the mouth. We could see the shank. Deftly he snipped the leader at the eye. The old fellow slipped back into the water, rested a minute or two, tentatively wriggled a fin, then, with a defiant flip of the tail, he surged downward into the blue caverns beneath. And that was that.

We laid to and took a little time to straighten things up again. It is surprising what an awful mess a boat gets into during a fight.

The wind had strengthened and the sea was a deep blue, flecked with white. Clemente was about three miles away. The surf was plain to see, a fringe of creamy white against the dark cliffs. We both felt pretty well pleased with ourselves. It was not noon yet and we had one fish to our credit already. Roy's morning grouch had fled away with the mists. From a silent, grumpy person he turned into a veritable chatterbox.

"That tickled me to death!" he exclaimed. "Your turnin' that fish loose! What th' hell was th' sense o' keepin' 'im? Most o' these here sports wanta pile 'em up like cordwood. I come across from here with fish that durn near stunk me off'n th' boat, they was so rotten. An' why for? Jus' so some bird could have his picture taken 'longside a string o' marlin. Didn't make no diff'rence if it took him two weeks to catch 'em!

"Now there's nobody likes to bring in fish any better'n me. That's my bread an' butter. Th' more fish I brings inter th' pier th' better chance I got o' bein' hired. But ther's times when tain't th' right thing to do. Take that bird we jus' cut loose. What good was he? We couldn't do nothin' with 'im. Jus' let him rot 'til he stunk so bad we'd have to dump 'im overboard. Th' way we done, one o' these here days he's goin' to fergit 'bout bein' hooked an' somebody else's gonna have some fun with 'im. I'm tellin' ya, I heard a lot 'bout these here sportsmen, but I ain't seen many. They squawk an' holler 'bout market fishin'. That's all right when market fishin' wipes th' fish out. I'm agin these big nets all th' time. Jus' th' same them sportsmen fergits that th' market fisherman eats, or don't eat, accordin' to whether he gits fish, or don't git 'em.''

He paused for breath, and a cigarette, and washed his hands in the bucket of sea water always standing ready. Glancing toward the island he grinned and went on.

"Bein' out here or hereabouts reminds me o' somethin' funny that happened a year or two ago.

"One o' Boschen's friends from Noo York come out here to git himself a marlin. Well, when he got to Av'lon th' fish was all over here an' Bosch was over here with 'em. He'd hired me to take care o' this bird an' bring him over. So I met him at th' steamer an' told him 'bout it an' that we'd come on over th' next mornin'.

"That was all right with him an' we come over. It was jus' 'bout here that I seen Bosch an' George hooked onto a fish. Thinkin' my party might like to see th' fun I edged over close to 'em.

"Well, you know how Bosch fights a fish. Stands up an' gives him hell all th' time. This time it looked like he was hooked onto somethin' 'bout as tough as he was! That fish wasn't gittin' no line off'n Bosch—but he was makin' damn sure Bosch wasn't gittin' none off'n him! I never see one put on such a show! He was goin' 'roun' th' *Mabel* like he was a grasshopper—out o' th' water more'n he was in! If there was anythin' that bird missed doin' I'd like to see it! First he walked on his tail, then he stood on his head! Next he jumped straight up in th' air an' looped th' loop! Then he'd come out, shoot twenty–thirty feet through th' air an' fifteen feet out! Twice't I thunk he was goin' to fly 'roun' th' *Mabel's* mast!

[27]

"I looked at my man an' his eyes was jus' poppin'. I told 'im that was Bosch. He kind o' nodded an' sez:

" 'What's that thing jumpin' 'round him?'

" 'That's a swordfish,' sez I. 'Watch him!'

" 'That's what I'm a doin',' sez he. 'Is there many o' them things 'round here?'

" 'Ocean's full of 'em,' sez I, thinkin' that'd make him feel good.

"He stares at that crazy fish a good five minutes, then turned to me an' sez:

" 'D' you mean to tell me that's what I've come all th' way from Noo York after?'

" 'Yessir,' sez I. 'An' we're goin' to git ourselves one, an' more'n one, too, th' way th' fish is runnin' over here.'

"He kind o' grunts. 'Like hell we are!' he snorts. 'Lissen here, Cap. You turn this here boat 'round an' git back to Av'lon fast as God'll let ya. T' hell with Boschen! There ain't nobody goin' to talk me inta gittin' aholt o' any damn thing like that!'

"An' he meant it, too! I tried t' argy, but it wa'n't no use. Back to Av'lon we went an' he tuk th' steamer over to th' mainland next mornin'—but not afore he'd left a note for Bosch tellin' what he thought of him! I thought old Bosch'd die a-laughin' when he read it!"

As a matter of fact, that is a true story.

We put out a new bait and chugged on toward the island for about a mile and a half, then turned and headed down toward the East End when we picked up The Fence. That Fence has always done something to me. It is part and parcel of Clemente. It is usually the place that we head for from Catalina—and our point of departure when we leave. And then it is so damned lonely looking! A fence post against the skyline, then a line of them marching down the steep slope of yellow wild oats—the last one seeming to hang precariously at the very brink of the cliff.

Down the coast we ran, slipping by the narrow little beaches, the dark canyons looking as though they might have been gouged out by some giant's hoe, the long sweeps of wild oats leading up to the sky. Magic fingers began to pluck at drowsy eyelids. The beat of the motor, the whisper of the sea, the warm sun, the salt wind, all conspired toward sleep. My head drooped. I jerked back into consciousness. Again it drooped. Those magic fingers were so gentle, so caressing—the world slipped away—

"SWISSSSSSH! CRAAAAASSSH! RRRRRRRRRRRR!"

I fumbled frantically at the rod, trying to get a firm grip on it.

Water boiled up under the stern as Roy went into reverse. The engine rattled and raced. A hundred feet of line whirred off the reel, then slowed and stopped. I threw on the drag and reeled fast until I came up against something heavy, solid. Then I struck hard, half a dozen times.

The surface parted and out leaped a slender, silver shape, its head wagging, its sword beating the air. As he leaped he threw the hook. I could see it shoot out of his mouth.

As I reeled in I felt a coldly disapproving eye fixed on my back. There was no use in stalling, so I turned around to take whatever was coming. Roy didn't say much, at first, but his expression was eloquent as he rigged on a fresh bait and tossed it overboard. Not until my line was out did he unburden himself. Even then it was short and to the point.

"Mebbe someday you'll learn ya can't go to sleep an' catch swordfish at th' same time!"

[29]

I didn't need to be told that—but those magic fingers had been very insidious. Now, however, they had fled far away, and I was alert for anything that might happen.

On, down coast, we worked. The lowering sun seemed to intensify the golden haze in which the whole island was bathed. The deep canyons turned into caverns of purple mystery. Sea birds, their day's hunting ended, flapped roostward.

"Look out!"

A purple shadow flashed by the teasers. An erect, dark fin cut the surface with a sound like ripping silk. Under the starboard one there was a boil, an eddying green swirl. The line jerked, then hung limp.

"Swisssssh!" That purple shadow flashed by the port one. Another boil, another swirl, another jerk, and that line hung limp.

"Swordfish! Swordfish!" I yelled—after it was all over. I never saw anything happen so fast in my life. One instant the sea had been empty. The next there were two boiling swirls and two teasers gone. And now the sea was empty again!

Grimly Roy pulled in the limp lines. Words must have failed him, for he only grunted, and tied on two new teasers.

Mosquito Harbor was abeam. We could see the white tents, smoke from the cookhouse, and three boats riding at anchor in the cove. One of them was Danielson's *Leta D.* which meant that Grey was over there. We talked over going in, then decided that we would rather go down to Smugglers'. On we went, past the Glory Hole, past Ghost Rock, past the Fish Hook, until Pyramid Head loomed above us and around the corner was Smugglers'. Big seas rolled in to crash in a smother of green and white upon the teeth of East End Reef. When we rounded the point we could see white flashes as the long surges flung themselves against the black rocks of China Point.

THE TUNA CLUB AT AVALON

Skirting the edge of the kelp beds we headed for the middle of the three terraced point that bisects the bay. I always like to head in there. It is like coming home. The day's work is ended. Peace and quiet and rest are just at hand.

Close to the kelp stretching out from the base of the middle terrace we rounded to. Roy throttled down the engine and ran up forward. There was a splash, the rattle of chain running through the hawse, then the sharp click as he checked it. The tide caught us, swinging us back until we came hard up against the anchor. He went below. There was a gurgle, a gasping cough and—quiet.

I went over to the rail and looked around. Inshore from us was a little jig boat. Its one man crew waved a friendly greeting. Further out lay a big purse seiner, drying clothing hanging from the forestay. The two shacks on the beach, the windmill, looked unutterably lonely.

Long seas rolled in from outside, lifting us gently, easily, then sliding out from under us to race shoreward and crash with the roar of thunder upon the steep beach.

I sat down in the chair and lit a cigarette. From below I could hear the clatter of pots and pans as Roy busied himself in the galley. Presently, up through the companionway floated the smell of boiling coffee.

Somewhere close to the black cliffs a sea lion barked. A startled sea gull scolded angrily back. The fog wind moaned its age old dirge through the rigging. A loose rope began to "tap-tap-tap-tap-tap-tap" against the mast. From around China Point, from out to sea, across the island, swept the streamers of fog. Silently, relentlessly they marched until we, and all around us, were lost in a world of veiled horizons.

[31]

"TUNA! TUNA!"

"TUNA! TUNA!" With those pulse stabbing words a veritable flood of memories sweeps over me, whirling me backward across the dimension of Time and into the past. I find myself, a little boy, standing wide-eyed upon the beach of Avalon Bay. The low surf crackles and whispers upon the shingle. Set along the curve of the crescent beach, just beyond the fingers of the tide, stand the flimsy booths of the boatmen. A lime streaked, weather beaten wharf stretches out into the waters of the bay. Upon it perch sea gulls, flapping their wings, hopping about, scolding querulously. One, serenely proud of his point of vantage, sits watchfully atop the derrick post. From the beach string lines of rowboats, some white, some green, some blue, some red, reminding one of decoys set and ready, awaiting the coming of their living brethren from out the grey skies. Behind is the little village—a very little village in those days—straggling haphazardly up the brown hillsides.

Standing at the very edge of the surf is a group of men. They stare fixedly out upon the bay, toward a rowboat that is slowly pulling shoreward, toward the despondent figure huddled in its stern sheets.

Slowly it crawls down a lane between the skiffs and runs up on the beach with a rasping crunch. The dejected figure in the stern, every effort betokening pain, straightens up and stares back at the silent group. Then, with a visible effort, he stands up and steps out, his shoes squelching unheeded in the wash of the tide. For an instant he staggers and rubs forehead and eyes with an elbow. The other hand is wrapped in a bloody, dirty bandage and he holds it tenderly against his body. His face is grey—lined with the lines of weariness and pain. Wearily he brushes past the interested group of watchers, shaking his head at the eager questions thrown at him, and stumbles on up the street to the ugly green bulk which is the Hotel Metropole.

Thus rebuffed the questioners hurl themselves upon the boatman. He has much to say, and says it with a wealth of gesture and frequent squirtings of tobacco juice.

As the story unfolds that group of listening men grows dejected too. It is a gloomy tale the boatman has to tell. That very morning, at daylight, the broken man who has just passed up the street was strong and proud, filled with joy of living, eager for the quest. From half a world away he had come to take with rod and reel a bluefin tuna. His chance had come—the fish were here. Confidently he had strode down the street and stepped into his waiting boat. Soon he would return—envied by all.

Return he did—but an object of pity rather than envy—a beaten, broken man. Out upon the battleground of the sea he had met King Tuna in fair and open fight—and had been soundly whipped for his pains!

Many other pictures of those old days come back to me. I see solid men, normally considered sane, rushing up and down the street, bidding five, ten, even twenty dollars for a single flying fish! I look out upon the channel and see the stabbing splashes, the breaking water, the milling birds, and great, dark shapes lunging clear as the schools of bluefin tuna go rolling up the channel. And I see, too, the wreckage they leave in their wake—the broken, splintered rods, the bruised and mangled hands—men stumbling wearily back to the sanctuary of their beds.

I venture as close as I dare to that holy of holies, that sacred corner of the wide verandah of the old Hotel Metropole where the anglers used to gather. I see them sitting there grim and hollow-eyed as they glumly compare their scars of battle—tell and re-tell the tales of long hours of gruelling struggle out upon the wide blue sea.

So it is, with such pictures before me, and with certain incidents which have happened with me in the years since, that there has grown up within me a most wholesome respect for old King Tuna. I readily grant that there are many, many splendid fighting fish in the waters of our world—broadbill, marlin, tarpon, sailfish, mako, yellowtail, albacore, steelhead, salmon, muskellunge, mahseer—the roster of them is long, and I respect them all and those who match their strength and skill against them. But of all the brotherhood of fighting fish I don't know where you will find the equal of the bluefin tuna for sheer gameness and never-say-die doggedness. And I promise you this—every one you get you will earn!

Perhaps I may be a little prejudiced on behalf of our Pacific bluefin tuna by reason of the method we must use to take them. I refer to kite fishing.

Years ago tuna would take a trolled bait. Then they stopped. For a long time we suffered the exasperation of trolling back and forth through school after school of splendid fish with not so much as the flash of a belly for our pains.

Then an Avalon boatman with a head upon his shoulders, George C. Farnsworth, invented the kite method. Study had led him to the theory that the bait must be put into the school before the wake of the boat had disturbed them. His theory was right, and to this day I don't know of any other way to get a Pacific bluefin tuna of any size to take a bait. The method is very simple and very interesting.

An ordinary square kite of silk is run up on three, four, five, or as many hundred feet of line as you fancy. We generally favor red silk—the silk because it is light and dries quickly, and red because it shows up well in the water. There are various methods of attaching the kite line to the fishing line, but the one I like best and have always used is the following: Use nine thread for the kite line. Unstrand the end that is away from the kite for two or three feet and *cut off* two of the strands. Tie the one that remains to the end swivel of the leader, or further up the fishing line if a strong wind makes it difficult to keep the bait in the water. Pay out about one hundred and fifty feet of fishing line and then put the boat on a course which will allow bait and kite to travel parallel to that course and preferably abeam or abaft the beam.

The result is most interesting. The kite pulls the bait along the *surface* in little skips and jumps and splashes. This action can be bettered by sweeps of the rod, technically known as "skipping the bait," making it jump through the air, sometimes twenty feet or more, to plop back with a splash.

When a school of tuna is sighted try to head them. Then cut across, skipping the bait as much as you can. If it jumps into the school before the wake of the boat gets there I promise you a smashing strike—and that is something for anybody's money.

Remember, the bait is on the surface. Tuna are sometimes pretty big. To get it they must come a good part of their length—sometimes all—out of the water and smash down upon it. Imagine the rise of a two or three pound trout, or bass, to a dry fly. Multiply that by fifty to a hundred, or more, and you get somewhat of a picture of what a tuna strike is like. The water splits open. A bronze torpedo lunges out. Down he crashes in a turmoil of white water. A

[36]

great green swirl eddies and spreads. Cutting the very center of it your line races down into the depths beneath. The jerk of the strike snaps the kite line and the kite flutters down to the surface. It is usually an easy matter to run over and pick it up before settling down to the business of fighting the fish.

Of one thing you may be very sure, however. If the wake of the boat reaches the school before the bait—or if it so much as reaches the leaders, those half dozen or so fish which scout ahead of every school of tuna, before the bait gets into the school—you will never, never get a strike. You can drag the bait through it, scrape it over their backs, hit them on the nose with it, and you will never get the flash of a belly. Every fish in that school is sinking and will not take a bait.

Two factors are fundamental to the success of kite fishing—tuna and wind. You can't catch fish unless they are there to catch, and you can't fly a kite without wind. And that brings to mind what Enos Vera, an Avalon boatman and an Azores Portuguese, once said.

It was an overcast morning off the east end of Catalina Island. The day offered promise. Everywhere we looked there were birds sitting upon the water. They were restless, too—sitting for a few moments, then lifting to fly a little way, then settling down again. That is a sign that something has been happening around there and is likely to happen again before long.

But there was not a breath of wind. The scarred cliffs of Catalina lifted up out of a grey sea and into a grey fog. A lazy swell rolled up out of the southwest. Here and there the glassy surface was broken by dark swirls, over which sea birds fought and screamed. Tuna were beginning to surface—but until the wind came they might as well have been upon the moon.

Back and forth we cruised, keeping close to the fish but not so close as to frighten them down. Both of us were sitting on top the cabin anxiously scanning the horizon for some hint of coming wind. There were other boats near us doing the same thing. One or two attempted to put up big kites, but the best they could do was to drag them and the bait along behind, which was worse than nothing.

Enos grew more and more fidgety as the dark swirls increased. At last he blew up.

"I tol' you, Mis' Bandin', thees here tunny fish she make-a me seek! You got lots o' ween', you no got no tunny. You got lots o' tunny, you no got no ween'. God damn thees tunny feesh!"

Right as rain, but there wasn't much we could do about it. By this time tuna were breaking water everywhere. There would be a flash of silver darts as bait leaped, and then, under them, dark boils of water and sharp, racing fins. It was maddening. Tuna are scarce enough at the best. But to have them all around us and not a chance to even have at them was a little too much. Of course they might stay up until the wind came. But then, again, they might not. It is either a very wise man, or a fool, who dares guess the comings and goings of tuna. One minute they may be everywhere, tearing the water white. The next, they may be gone. Today the ocean is literally alive with them. Tomorrow it is as empty as a poor man's pocketbook.

Suddenly Enos stood up and peered intently for two or three minutes into the southwest. Then he turned and grinned.

"Ween' she come!" he announced and climbed down off the cabin.

Yes—there it was—a dark line upon the horizon. Thank Heaven!

By the time we were ready the first puffs reached us. Enos climbed up on the rail and tossed the big red kite into the air. For an instant it swayed and darted, threatening to dive into the sea, then, as another puff caught it, it bellied and sailed up and away from us. The stranded end of the kite line was tied to the leader and the bait tossed overboard. The kite bobbed and swooped as it felt the weight of the dragging flying fish. Enos turned down wind a trifle. The kite sank. The bait levelled down upon the surface. The fishing line dragged in a bow. Then a stronger gust caught the square of red silk. It leaped higher, straightening out the slack, lifting the bait. For a moment the flying fish hung inert and lifeless, then, after an astonishingly life-like wriggle, leaped ahead. Not ten feet in front of its nose the water parted under three or four boiling swirls.

"Skip 'im!" Enos yelled. "Oh, skip 'im!"

I swept the rod backward in a wide arc. The bait leaped high in the air and shot forward, to fall with a sousing splash. A swift shadow shot under it. Again I jerked. The bait started to leap again. The water burst open and out lunged a maddened tuna. Down he smashed square upon the bait. White water flew high. The swirl eddied and spread. I jerked a third time, coming up against something heavy, solid. The kite line snapped. The kite fluttered down. The stout hickory rod doubled almost to the water's edge.

"STRIKE! STRIKE! RRRRRRRRRRRRRRRRRR!"

The big reel broke into its battle song. Away went the line, so fast the spinning spool was nothing but a blur. I hurriedly backed off the drag and turned anxiously to see what Enos was doing.

I knew it! There he was, leaning way over the side reaching for something—the kite. I never saw a boatman yet who wouldn't risk almost anything to recover a $2.50 kite. Or, maybe, they aren't taking the chances the angler thinks.

"Get after him!" I shouted. "Hurry up! He's taking too much line!"

Enos never hurried in his life, but, soon enough, he slipped into reverse. The strain eased and as we picked up speed I began to recover line. Soon we were almost straight over him and there was no more line to be recovered—at least then. I glanced at the half empty spool and groaned. Long ago I had learned the lesson that only by sweat of the brow and pain of the body could those hundreds of feet be spooled in.

Well, there we were—he at one end and I at the other. For a minute or two we tugged and strained against each other, then he began his great, boring circles. I braced my feet, set up the drag, and went to work. Pump and reel—pump and reel—pump and reel—until every joint, muscle, tendon and nerve seems to scream with torture—until sweat pours off you—pours into your eyes, blinding you—until you become one great pain. The fish is deep down. There he intends to stay if he can. Only by unrelenting pumping and reeling, lifting and dropping, picking up the slack as you drop, can you ever lift him.

I tugged and strained. The wet handgrip slipped in my grasp. When the circles came toward the boat I gained a few feet—or inches. When they bore away the tip doubled downward and I lost almost as much as I had gained—sometimes more. Never for a single instant dare you relax when fighting a tuna. If you do—if you try to seize a moment to breathe deeply, to flex and unflex your cramped hands—God help you! Your fish will likewise relax and rest—and he will come back far quicker than you. It is dogged does it in tuna fishing. There is no fast reeling to pick up slack. After the first mad rush there are no long runs. The boat seldom has to be moved when

fighting a tuna, except once, perhaps, if the fish comes too far forward in one of his circles. No, tuna fishing—all big game fishing, for
that matter, has plenty of hard work mixed in with the fun one gets
out of it.

I glanced at my watch. Fifteen minutes. It seemed more like an
hour! I looked around. Other boats were working back and forth—
or rushing full speed toward boiling swirls. Over each sailed the little square of red that marked the kite. One or two were hooked on.
I could see the anglers pumping, the flash of sun on varnished rods.
A boat passed us about three hundred yards off. There was a big
splash alongside. The kite jerked—then fluttered downward. Another one hooked on! I just started to congratulate myself that I was
better off than the other fellow, having about twenty minutes of my
fight behind me, when

"RRRRRRRRR! RRRRRRRRR! RRRRRRRR!"

The snarl of the reel brought me back to stern realities. Unconsciously I had relaxed—and my fish had taken full advantage of it.
Yards of hard earned line lost in the twinkling of an eye.

Back to the grind I went. Pump and reel—pump and reel—
pump and reel. That moment of relaxation had brought new life to
the fish—new stubbornness—new strength. It was another twenty
minutes before I felt even reasonably certain that once again I had
the upper hand of him.

The circles widened—and shallowed. Little by little he was being forced toward the surface. A wide circle swung toward us. Enos
leaned over the rail, peering down.

"There she is!" he cried. "I see 'im. She good fish!"

I tried looking over for myself but found that I had too much to
attend to. The fish was stubbornly contesting every inch. I glanced

at the reel. There was very little line out—fifty feet, perhaps. He swung out wide. Now I could see him in the swells, a shimmering bulk of greenish blue.

Sight of the boat seemed to have frightened him. He lay out there and struggled desperately, twisting this way and that. Then, without a second's warning he whirled and rushed across our stern. I was hard put to it to get out of the chair in time to pass the rod around to save the line from fouling rudder or propeller.

Once on the other side of us he tried hard to get his head on me —and only missed by a hair! For a few minutes—it seemed half an hour—it was even-Stephen. The line sang like a banjo string. He was close aboard—close enough to screw up the drag as tight as it would go and thumb down hard on the line. The hickory tip bent to a dangerous arc, but that couldn't be helped. It was one of those many do-or-die occasions which arise when one is fighting a big fish. If ever he got the best of me at that point, it would be hours before I would have him as close—if at all.

He could be seen plainly, just under the surface, rolling, twisting, writhing, fighting. Even under the tension of that few minutes' struggle I experienced the thrill I always feel at sight of a fighting tuna. Their bodies are so powerful looking, and yet so clearly built for speed, that there is something about them that seems to set them apart from any other fish.

At last the strain told. His head swung toward us. I pumped fast. The swivel came out—then bobbed under as the fish surged down. Enos was at the rail, gaff ready, hand outstretched. Again the swivel came out, hung an instant and jerked under again. A third time it came out. The fish rolled on his side. Now was my chance. Putting every ounce I had left into it I pumped in those last four or five feet and swung the tip toward Enos. He grabbed the swivel, made a quick pass with the gaff—and there was a heavy thumping alongside—a bucketful of water slopped over the rail. Even on the gaff the fish was fighting hard!

"Gimme rope!" Enos shouted. "Gimme rope!"

I had gotten out of the chair, backed off the drag—to be ready for any eventuality—so it was an easy matter to snatch up the piece of rope with the noose in it, which should be always ready for just such an occasion, and hand it to him. But even then, with the two of us working, it was no easy matter to get that noose around the tail. Only when that has been successfully accomplished can one be sure of a fish.

Between the two of us we dragged him up over the rail and lashed him down—and still he thumped and beat the deck. He looked a good fish—perhaps a hundred and ten pounder.

For the next few minutes we were pretty busy. In the first place there was blood everywhere. Tuna bleed like pigs. That mess has to be cleaned up, which means sloshing countless buckets of water upon the deck, along the rail, in the cockpit, wherever blood has splattered. If you don't get it cleaned up while it is fresh, it won't be long before the boat smells like a charnel house. The kite line, which has been pulled in and just dropped somewhere where it will be out of the way, has to be untangled—I never knew it to fail to get into an ungodly snarl—and whatever can be saved from it spooled back on a reel. Then, as a rule, the engine has to be oiled. That takes about five or ten minutes. A fresh kite must be run up and another bait hooked on. All in all one can figure on about twenty minutes of fussing around before getting back to fishing.

By the time we had done everything that had to be done those dark swirls had gone—the tuna had disappeared—the boats scattered, each following his own hunch as to where they might pop up next. Even the birds were gone. It has always been one of the mysteries of tuna fishing to me the way fish can disappear. One minute the ocean is alive with them, the air is full of screaming, milling birds—the next, there is not a sign of either fish or birds.

Well, no matter—"maskee" as the Chinese say. One hundred-pound tuna is enough for any man in one day. How much better hunting and fishing we would all have today if we would only be satisfied with one good fish, or with only what game we can use, but we won't and never will be.

Of course we, just like all the rest of them out there, whether lucky or otherwise, fished the day out. But the fish were gone. A nasty sea built up. So, early in the afternoon, we gave up fighting the Clemente Channel and went home.

Oh, yes—I forgot. The fish weighed 123 pounds, 7 ounces.

There is another day, perhaps afternoon would be better, spent with tuna, which I know I shall never forget as long as I live.

There was—and is—a man named James W. Jump, "Jimmie Jump," who is a *great* angler. In all Southern California waters his broad-beamed, able launch *Ranger* is as well known as are the islands. As a rule his son Rob acts as his boatman. Between them they have caught a lot of fish and established many Tuna Club records.

In the summer of 1923 something happened to Rob. I don't remember what it was, but he couldn't run the boat and Jim asked me if I would come over to Avalon and help him out. Of course I was glad to—or at least I was until I got over there and found out how things were.

[44]

"TUNA! TUNA!"

Jim was literally "fish hungry." Everything had broken badly for him all summer. As a matter of fact they hadn't been breaking any too well for anybody. Tuna were scarcer than the proverbial hens' teeth. As empty days rolled into empty weeks tempers frayed. Lifelong friends found themselves snarling at one another. Anglers damned their boatmen—boatmen damned their anglers. That often is the case in this game of fishing. It is no soft touch to fight rough water day in and day out—with not even the chance of a fish for your efforts. One thing should be borne in mind regarding our fishing out here: We have to go out into the open sea after them. We have no big sheltered bays or inlets. Our channels are rough—particularly the San Clemente. But, rough or not, there is where the fish are, and there we have to go.

As far as I was concerned I didn't particularly care whether we caught any fish or not. Long before I had learned to find just as much joy in cruising the ocean, watching its ever-changing face, watching the bird life, the cloud effects, the lonely islands humping up over the horizon, as I had in the mere act of catching fish. Furthermore, I had found it good fun to handle a boat for someone else when he was on a fish.

But with Jump it was different. He wanted fish, wanted them badly, and was getting thoroughly tired of the empty days. Within a day or two I found his state of mind influencing mine—and *my* temper growing short, too. I don't believe I ever worked so hard to find fish—yet didn't find them!

One evening, after a particularly bad day of threshing around the Clemente Channel, I went down to the Pleasure Pier to see if there was any news there. There was always the chance that some market fisherman might have run into fish somewhere where we hadn't been. But there was nothing doing. The boatmen on the pier were growling just as loud as the anglers at the Tuna Club.

On the way back I met George Farnsworth. You will find that name cropping up from time to time through these pages. If anybody knows fish, or where they are likely to be found, it is George. On the other hand he is exceedingly close-mouthed. To ask him questions is but a waste of time and breath. If he does tell one anything it is only when he feels like doing so.

We stopped and chatted a few minutes about nothing in particular. Then he rolled his cigar and cocked one eye at me.

"See anything today?" he asked.

"No—nothing except a lot of ocean."

For a minute or two he kept on rolling that infernal cigar and half-grinning at me.

"Well," he said at last, almost casually, "I was up off the West End today. Just a kind of picnic party. There are lots of big tuna up there. Well—so long," and he turned on his heel and went down the street, leaving me staring and speechless.

"West End—lots of big tuna up there!" I couldn't believe my ears!

I had a good deal of trouble getting Jump out of the locker room and away where I could talk to him. And when I did, and when I told him what I had heard, he didn't warm up much.

"Just kiddin' you," was his comment. "Nothin' would tickle George more than to send us off on a long boat ride. Probably laughin' up his sleeve at you now!"

I didn't think so and said so.

"All right! All right!" he snapped. "Have it your own way! We might as well go up there as any place, I guess. There ain't no damn fish anywhere. One thing, though. Up there we'll be away from these other cusses!"

"I saw a market fisherman tonight," he added, just to show that he wasn't being contrary for contrariness' sake. "He just come down from Osborne Bank. Said he hadn't seen anything."

That is one of the secrets of Jim's success in fishing. He has more contacts with those who take their living out of the sea than any man I ever knew. There is very little that goes on within a hundred and fifty miles of Avalon that he doesn't hear about.

The next morning he was as skeptical as ever. As I rowed alongside the *Ranger* he came up from below in his undershirt and trousers.

"S'pose you're still hell bent on goin' up to th' West End?" he grumbled, polishing his glasses. "I'd kind of figured on goin' out toward the East End of Clemente today. Takes three hours to go up to the West End—and three hours to come back. That leaves 'bout fifteen minutes for fishin'."

I knew what was in his mind. He was looking for a goat in case Farnsworth *had* sent us on a wild goose chase—or in case we found nothing. For once I was willing to be that goat.

"Yeah," I replied, climbing aboard and making the skiff fast to the bow line. "That's where we're going!" And went below to oil up the engine.

It *is* a long way in a slow boat from Avalon to the West End—a good eighteen or nineteen miles before you clear the island. And it is another ten or fifteen miles to where you are likely to find fish—if any are to be found at all.

The sky was overcast—the usual high fog of California's summers. The sea was as smooth as glass except for a lazy northwest roll.

We slid along Catalina's rugged coast, its bold headlands sheltering peaceful coves, its inviting valleys leading back into the main ranges. In due time the Isthmus opened, with its row of eucalyptus trees against a sky line, hinting of countless leagues of lonely sea beyond.

Off the West End the ocean stretched away into fog—grey, lifeless and cold. Not much of promise there. Jim was glum and silent. After a while he fell asleep in the chair.

There wasn't much wind, but enough to fly a kite after a fashion, so I ran one up and put a bait out, lashing the rod to a fishing chair. Then I headed northwest for about ten or twelve miles before I swung off to southward in a big circle. There was absolutely no life to be seen except an occasional high-flying gull, a shearwater, a shark, or once in a while a flying fish driven out from under our bows.

About noon Jim woke up, got up, stretched himself, squinted around the horizon, and climbed up on the rail.

"Seen anything?" he asked. "No? All right—let's have something to eat. I'll take her."

When I came back with coffee and sandwiches he had plenty to say. He had had time to see what I had been seeing all morning— the general emptiness of that cold looking ocean. Besides, Jim is no fool. He knows as much about the sea and fish and signs as anybody.

"Satisfied now?" he demanded, biting into a sandwich. "Nice day up here! Nice boat ride! You're as bad as Rob! B'lieve anything them damned devils tell you! I had a reason for wantin' to go toward Clemente. Fellow telephoned me last night from Pedro. A purse seiner come in from there with tuna!"

"Why in hell didn't you say so?" I demanded, getting mad.

"Humph! What'd been th' use? If we had gone over there and hadn't found 'em you'd never of quit bellyachin' 'bout it. Mebbe so

we're just as well off up here as any place. There ain't no tuna anywhere. Anybody that says so's a damn liar."

Lunch eaten, we both climbed on top the cabin. The sun had begun to break through and the wind was freshening. Somehow or
other the sea didn't look so empty.

Just a little way off the port bow a bunch of bait popped up. The
way they came out looked to me as though something were after
them. A shark, probably, but I swung the *Ranger* so that our bait
would cross the spot, or thereabouts. Jim wouldn't listen to me when
I suggested that he get down to the rod just in case.

"To hell with it!" he snapped.

The flying fish wriggled, skittered and jumped ahead, landing
just about where the bait had come out.

"*Pow! Craaash!*" The water exploded and out came one of the
biggest tuna I had ever seen.

Three times he lunged and three times he missed. Both of us had
scrambled down off the cabin and Jim was struggling with the rod
lashings. Again the fish—or his twin—jumped and missed, crushing the bait to pulp.

That's what comes of doing something else other than fishing
when you are out fishing. Jim reeled in fast. Fortunately the kite had
not broken off and I had another bait ready. Suddenly I heard him let
out a yell.

"My God! Look at 'em!"

I looked up—and then *I* yelled. Everywhere, all around us, as
far as we could see in every direction, the water was torn white by
feeding tuna! Sardines, anchovies, mackerel, flying fish shot into the
air like silver rain. Under them great bronze backs, sharp fins, raced
and tore. Birds came rushing to the kill. Even above the rattle and

chug of the engine we could hear the crash of breaking water as the great fish lunged out, the ripping sound of fins cutting the surface, the high pitched screams of blood-maddened sea birds.

I thought I would *never* get that new bait hooked on—but at last I did, and tossed it overside. Jim let the reel run free. I don't believe the bait was twenty feet away from us when there was a smashing strike and the tip jerked downward.

"*Got him!*" Jim yelled.

I started to swing toward the kite—then swung back again. That kite, as soon as a couple of hundred feet of line were in the water, was racing away to leeward. But that was all right. Kites are cheap. Tuna aren't.

Jim went to work as only he can. Smoothly, rhythmically, every move counting, he pumped and reeled. With one eye on the line where it entered the water I busied myself sewing up as many baits as I could. Something told me we would need them.

"Here he is!" I heard.

I jumped to the rail, gripped the swivel—it was ready and waiting for me—and gaffed the fish. On board he appeared to be well over a hundred. While Jim lashed him down I put up another kite and looked around. The fish were gone!

But no—they weren't. There they were, half a mile to windward. They were moving fast, those tuna.

When we caught up with them again the bait had barely brushed the edges of them before the water boiled again and out lunged three or four fish after it.

"*Got him!*"

Again the kite went to glory. The wind was piling up every minute. I ran below for smaller ones and found to my horror that there wasn't a single one aboard smaller than the big thirty-six-inch light weather ones. Well—there wasn't anything to do about it. Gathering up an armful—all there were—I scrambled back on deck again just in time to hear,

"*Here he is!*"

I rubbed the sweat out of my eyes. Here we were with two fish on board already—both considerably better than hundred pounders—and millions of fish in sight. I pinched myself to see if I was dreaming.

"Next one's yours," Jim said, wiping the salt off his glasses as I threw up another kite.

It was nice of him, but I wouldn't have dreamed of touching the rod that afternoon. Only once or twice in a lifetime does a man get into fish as we were. Jim was getting along. The days of his fishing were nearing their end. As for me, I had long years before me. Let this be *his* big day! (Strangely enough, Jim is still fishing—and getting them—while I haven't touched a rod for six years and never will again. That shows just how far ahead we can see. But if it was to be done all over again, and if I knew what was ahead, I still would have done as I did.)

The minute the wind caught that big kite it simply leaped into the air, jerking the bait fifty feet above the surface. I headed down wind and Jim threw off the drag. Between the two of us we managed to plunk it back into the water.

"*Got him!*"

Another kite went the way of his fellows. The last I saw of it was a tiny speck of red. Where they all went to I don't know, unless they crashed against the cliffs of Catalina fifteen miles away.

Five minutes of hard pumping and reeling and number three

was gaffed, hauled aboard and tied down. In the excitement I don't think either of us quite realized what was happening. We have talked about it lots of times since. There we were, all by ourselves, not a boat in sight, and the sea actually boiling with hundred-pound tuna! I think we both went a little crazy. Jim shouted and sang. I blew the whistle until the air tanks were empty. Even the placid old *Ranger* did a little dancing about. In fact, she did more than dance. She stood on her head, then on her tail, and rolled her rails down in between. One big sea caught us, hurling the both of us, and the ice box, and a couple of chairs, down into one corner of the cockpit where water boiled up through the self-bailers. But we didn't care.

I never saw fish travel so fast. By the time we had hooked and landed one it took us twenty minutes to half an hour to catch up with the schools again. Up to windward big black clouds were piling. The wind was really blowing—and getting stronger every minute. Big seas were lumping up. Water slopped over the rail constantly. The cockpit deck was slippery with blood and salt water. There hadn't been a minute's time for a proper clean up.

The fourth kite started straight up to Heaven. Even with running down wind, and with the drag free, the closest we could get the bait to the water was about ten feet. Right then something happened which I have never seen before or since. The surface split open and *straight up into the air leaped a huge tuna*. With one convulsive twist he looped over and nailed that bait. We both yelled. Who wouldn't? Just think of it. He took a bait a good ten feet in the air!

"Got him!"

I don't yet know how Jim did what he did. There must have been all of seven hundred feet of line out when the fish struck and I know he must have taken another three hundred in his run. He was a big fish—bigger than two hundred pounds if we were any judges, and we had seen him in the air, mind you. And there he was, big as all outdoors and with a thousand feet of line out. I just kissed him good-bye.

I never saw such rod work in my life. Of course I headed down toward the fish at as good a rate as I dared and yet keep the line from bowing. But I needn't have worried. Jim picked up line as fast as I could recover it for him with the boat. The rod swept in wide arcs. Never once did he attempt to crank in the slack. Instead, just at the right split second he struck the crank with his hand, spinning in the slack. That is a trick I have never seen any other angler use. Try it some time. Great gashes cut through the water. Yards piled up with each sweep. In less time than the telling takes we were over that fish and up solid against him. Then Jim really went to work. He had to. Here was a very different breed of cats from the others. For all of twenty minutes it was just see-saw back and forth. But at last the strain began to tell. He pumped and reeled furiously. The hundred-foot marker came out, hung a moment then shot up to the tip and down the rod. I got the gaff ready and leaned over the side. Waves half drowned me, but deep down I could see that shimmer of green-blue. As it came closer the bulk of him simply amazed me. Even allowing for the distortion of water he appeared to be twice as big as anything we had aboard so far.

Jim was working steadily but carefully now—watching every sea, taking whatever advantage of them he could. The swivel came out, bobbed under, came out again, and then seemed to jump toward the tip. Jim swung toward me.

"Careful now!" he warned.

I reached out and got a firm grip on the swivel. The fish was surging heavily. I swayed back on him to bring him a little closer—to make sure of a more certain gaff. He was very heavy—the heaviest tuna I have ever held on a leader. He pulled me back, surging downward. The *Ranger* started to lift over a sea. A cross sea caught us and twisted our stern over. There was a sickening jerk and I sprawled back into the cockpit. I had pulled out the hook!

"Damn" was all Jim said. Later he told me that he hadn't the heart to say more as I stood there holding the empty leader in my hand and staring at it foolishly.

Well—that was that. It was my fault and mine alone. I should have let the leader go when those seas boarded us—or I should have reached out and gaffed the fish without trying to be so particular about having him just where I wanted him. I should have done a dozen things except what I did do. But—oh, well—that's the hell of fishing. Every so often you do the wrong thing. Unfortunately it is always at a time when doing the right thing would mean everything in the world. There will never be any question in either of our minds but that that was a Tuna Club record, would have beaten the two-hundred-fifty-one pounder that has hung on the wall for forty years!

There wasn't much said after that tragedy. The heart was out of both of us. I re-rigged and we caught up with the fish and got two more. But they were mere hundred pounders.

It was growing late. The sun was sinking, angry red, through masses of black cloud. The seas were getting worse all the time. Astern lay Catalina, a brooding, indistinct mass—and with miles of yeasty water between us. Jim pulled out his watch and looked at it. Then he looked at the still feeding fish—at the sinking sun—at the shouting seas—and back at his watch again.

"Well," he announced, throwing his rod down to the deck, "I guess we better be gettin' out o' here. It's better'n forty miles to Av'lon, kid—and it'll take us six hours to get there. Head her about!"

As I swung the wheel I took one last look. There they were, leaping, surging, feeding, racing away to windward into that angry, wind-swept sunset. Neither we, nor anybody else, ever saw those fish again.

Author's Note: Since writing this chapter Jimmie Jump has taken the Long Traverse down to those Mystic Seas. Good fishin' to you, Jim—and God bless you.

R. B.

AVALON OVER 50 YEARS AGO

MORE TUNA

SOMEHOW or other I never seem to tire of talking about tuna fishing. There is some intangible thing about it that makes it stand out from all else. Perhaps it is the kite—perhaps the flying fish bait skittering and jumping along, leaping the crest of a sea to splash down into the hollow beyond—perhaps it is the concentrated ferocity of the smashing strike of a big tuna. Or perhaps it is a little of all these things—and other things thrown in for good measure—I don't know. But I know I like it—and I like to talk about it. Scenes from those years of tuna fishing flicker across the memory as a motion picture flickers across the screen. True, they are broken sequences. Some are startlingly clear. Others are vague, blurred, only half seen. But, with every frame, whether clear cut, or shadowy, there comes a little stab of the pulse.

I was fishing out of Avalon with the late Major Lawrence Mott. There were a lot of small fish coming in, sixty to eighty pounds, but the hundred pounders weren't to be had. One morning Lawrie and I thought we would prospect new waters, so we headed out North Northeast toward Newport Bay.

The day promised to be nasty. By eight o'clock there was a stiff northwest wind bucking a southeast swell—the latter rolling up from a storm somewhere down south along the coast of Baja California. Any seaman knows what that means—a nasty, sloppy sea with a twisting cross chop thrown in for good measure. It was bad fishing weather and yet—one never could tell.

The little *Mabel* rolled and pitched and bucked like a mad thing.

The wind was cold. Even the water seemed to bite as it slopped aboard and doused us. My son, Bud, who was along, was as sick as a dog. But he was game. When I insisted on turning back and putting him ashore he raised such a fearful row that I gave up the idea. Mott and I huddled in the lee of the cabin for such shelter as we could find. The kite was up, the bait out, and the rod lashed to the chair.

Instead of getting better it got worse. About half-past ten we passed four battleships out for practice. Even they were rolling until they showed their red underbodies. I asked myself what business we had out in weather that made a battle wagon roll! But we kept on going—grousing, of course, about the weather, and talking about going in for the day—but doing nothing about it.

About half-past eleven—we could see the oil derricks at Huntington Beach—Mott let out a yell. A big tuna boiled up just astern of the bait. Three times he lunged and missed as I tore frantically at the lashings. I had just freed the rod and was into the chair when he leaped clear and smashed down squarely upon it.

Down he plunged—almost straight down. Mott had gone into reverse to ease the strain but had to get out of it again in a hurry lest we cut the line on the propeller. The kite simply sailed away to glory.

I backed the drag all the way off. That run was making me nervous. There was too much line out—and too straight down for such a sea. I looked at Mott and shook my head. He grinned.

"Stay with him," he encouraged. "He's bound to quit pretty soon now."

Maybe so—but there were no signs of it yet. The sight of the dwindling line, the shouting crested seas, the knowledge of what it meant to pump back that much line in that kind of water, filled me with despair.

[58]

Well, there was nothing to do but hang on and pray. I think we anglers flatter ourselves when we say we stop a tuna. I don't think we do anything of the kind. I think they stop themselves. There comes a time when the drag of the line through the water becomes too much for even such splendid strength and speed as theirs, and they gradually slow down and stop—or else the line breaks.

At last, and when I had about given up hope, *this* run slowed and stopped and changed into great, boring circles. That is one of the qualities I like in tuna. When they have reached their ultimate limit by rushing they still keep boring downward.

Ordinarily, when a tuna's run has stopped, there are a few minutes when you don't do much fighting. Instead, the boat works over toward the fish and you content yourself with picking up the more or less slack line. But here was an exception to the general rule. As I said before, that fish had plunged almost straight down. At the end of his run we were right on top of him. Moving the boat away a little was of no avail. We only lost more line. There was nothing for it but to pump and reel as best I could, fighting desperately for every inch. And, of course, the big seas didn't help any.

The fish was circling, but what circles they were! When he swung away from us I couldn't hold him to save me—and when he swung in he circled so far forward that Mott had to kick the boat ahead to prevent fouling him. As a result I not only lost line when I could expect to lose it, but lost it when I should have picked up some. I glanced at my watch. Half an hour had gone by. That is a long time, too long, for an ordinary hundred pounder. Mott had been declaring that we had hooked a very big fish and I began to think he was right.

I tightened up a little more and worked all the harder, cussing

Mott out every time he moved ahead, although the Lord knows he couldn't help it. But it was maddening to lose line when I should have been getting it.

After a time we both—the fish and I—began to feel the strain. With me it took the form of assorted aches and pains. But with him it meant beginning to give to that never ending pressure. Wet line piled up on the reel.

Mott danced about like a crazy man. "Get that fish in! Get that fish in!" he kept yelling.

A quick glance around told me the reason. The sea was literally alive with big tuna. Even a mile or more away could be seen the flash of their bellies as they slid down the swells.

Perhaps the sight gave me second wind—perhaps the fish had fought himself out. Whatever the reason I began to get line by feet and yards. Mott got his gaff ready. He and Bud, who had forgotten all about seasickness when the strike came, hung over the side peering down into the depths below.

"There he is!" they both shouted in chorus.

"Golly, he's a whopper!" Mott added, coming aft beside me. "Take plenty of time. Let's not make any mistakes now."

But right about there the fish stuck and refused to budge. Perhaps he had seen the boat and didn't care for it. I strained and heaved for all I was worth. The heavy hickory buckled almost to the water's edge. The line quivered under the strain, flicking off drops of water to form miniature rainbows.

Then he started rushing back and forth across the stern. That is just plain hell on the angler! There is but one thing to do. Get out of the chair, get the butt into a belt socket, or between your legs, or wherever you *can* get it and run back and forth across the stern with him, holding the rod as far out over the stern as you can and with the tip down into the water. Mott tried to run away from him but he clung to us like a leech. If I shuffled and scrambled across that stern once, I did it fifty times before he let up.

Then he started boring down and away from us. But he couldn't stand that long and surfaced, rolling in the swells about seventy-five feet off to starboard. He was a beautiful sight, a shimmering green-blue. And he was very, very tired—half on his side—a sure sign with a tuna that he is almost done. But even then, dog tired as he was, it took every ounce of strength I had to pump him over close enough for Mott to make the gaff.

With his shout, "I've got him!" I glanced at my watch. An hour and fifteen minutes.

We dragged him on deck and measured him. To those who don't know, it might be of interest to learn how that is done. Multiply the square, in inches, of the greatest girth, by the length, in inches, measuring from the tip of the upper jaw to the crotch of the tail, and being careful to square it, not to follow the contour of the body, and divide by 800. By this method one can ascertain the weight of a tuna to an ounce. This one measured exactly 135 pounds—a good fish.

By this time I had had all the tuna fishing I wanted for that day —but Mott thought otherwise. So did Bud.

We cleaned up the mess and looked around. There were still lots of tuna—but none very close. Mott rigged up another kite and bait while I seized the chance for a sandwich and cup of coffee. Before I was half finished he thrust the rod into my hands with the admonition to "Hop to it!"

I was just letting out the bait—it wasn't fifty feet off—when a shadow darted under it.

"Skip it!" Mott yelled. "He's after it! Skip it!"

I jerked. The bait leaped into the air and smacked back.

"SWISSSSH! CRAAAAASH!" A bronze shape lunged to smash down with a heavy splash and a turmoil of broken water.

"*Strike!*" I yelled—and hit him hard.

The throaty snarl of the reel turned into a higher pitched scream under one of the most astonishing tuna runs I have ever seen.

Instead of plunging downward this fish took off along the surface with the speed of an express train. His sharp fins cutting the water, the shine of his wide back, the wake he made, all were in plain sight. I don't believe my line touched the surface for at least three hundred feet. He was racing away to windward. The kite had broken off and was sailing off to leeward, just as had the other.

Mott had acted very quickly and swung the *Mabel* almost before the fish got under way. As a result we were able to follow him bow on. Otherwise, at the speed he was going, there wouldn't have been a chance. Even as it was, running wide open at nine knots, he was taking line.

That furious, and unusual, surface run lasted for all of fifteen minutes. Then he slowed down a bit and plunged downward. Deep down as far as he could go, dragging all that heavy line, it was almost as though he had tossed out an anchor and set himself, leaving us to do the worrying. And we worried plenty—or, at least, I did. There was twice as much line out as was safe. There was a wretched sea running. I was already pretty tired from the other fight.

For half an hour I gave him everything I had—and I don't think I pumped back fifty feet. Pretty soon I began to wonder. I had been whipped by a lot of fish—but always through their getting away someway or other. Never had I given up and turned the rod over to someone else. But this time I wasn't sure what would happen. My hands were already cramped and blistered, the muscles and tendons of my forearms sore. The rod twisted and slipped in my grasp. I couldn't seem to get a grip on it. Footing was slippery from water that dripped off the rod and slopped over the side. The *Mabel*, of course, was rolling frightfully—one always gets into the trough when fighting a fish and usually stays there. Mott made me doubly nervous by keeping up a never ending chatter that the "fish is twice as big as the other" and "For God's sake don't lose him!" At last I told him to shut up. I had troubles enough as it was!

Just as I was being convinced against my will that I had reached the ultimate end, that I couldn't lift another ounce, the strain eased and the tip jerked upward. He had had enough too. Strength seemed to flow back in a flood. Aches and pains disappeared. I pumped and reeled for all I was worth. Wet line piled up on the reel. Faster and faster, more easily, it came in—yards at a time. The spot where it entered the water kept moving away from us. He was surfacing. Again an unusual thing for a tuna to do.

The hundred foot marker came out. Mott and Bud both yelled. Off to starboard, rolling like a log in the steep seas, was a blue-green bulk. Every second there came a flash of a silver belly. He was dead —or nearly so.

Very carefully we worked over toward him. A fish is always dangerous when he is rolling on the surface a little way off. I don't know how many I have lost at that very point through overeagerness, or overconfidence—but there are three or four that I refuse to even think about.

The swivel came out. Mott grabbed it and pulled the fish alongside. He was as dead as a herring.

We pulled him on board and laid him beside the other. Side by side he didn't look "twice as big"—but he certainly looked a third larger. We didn't even bother to measure him. I wish we had!

Mott started to rig up another bait but I shook my head.

"Nothing doing," I told him, tenderly nursing my blistered hands. "I've had all I want. We're going home."

Now comes a part of this story that I have never been able to figure out. I have said that the second fish, laid alongside the first, appeared clearly to be a third again as large, perhaps a half. He was longer—he was thicker. There wasn't the shadow of a doubt in either of our minds but that, if our measurement of the first one had been correct—and we were certain it was—this one weighed close to two hundred pounds. So sure was I that I didn't even bother to watch the weighing and had Mott let me off at the Tuna Club before taking the fish over to the Pleasure Pier. When he called me up to tell me the weights I was speechless. The first one weighed 131 pounds, the second 132! Even Murphy, the famous old rod-maker, who had seen the fish lying side by side, couldn't believe his ears when he was told. That incident only goes to show how far wrong the best of us can be when it comes to guessing at the weight of fish. I can't help wondering how many big fish I have been hooked on to, and lost, weren't nearly as big as I thought.

"Fishing Luck." What worlds of exultation—of bitter disappointment—are contained in that well worn phrase. "Fishing Luck!" Who can guess what it will bring? Why, with two men sitting in the same boat, using the same bait, the same tackle, does it bless the one and avoid the other? One never knows when it will strike, or when it does if it will be good or bad. And it is a strange thing—or so it has been with me—that it is the bad luck which has remained most vividly in my memory.

All of us who fish must take the bitter with the sweet. As I look back over the years and count up the tally of what I am pleased to call "bad luck" I find a great part of it not to have been "luck" at all—but rather my own fault. And I think that is the kind that hurts the most. No one should complain when soundly whipped in a fair fight. One has had one's chance, and not been man enough to win. That's the game. But to toss good chances away through one's own damn foolishness, that is something else again. God knows, the tally of such incidents during my fishing makes me hide my face in shame! And yet, if one comes down to facts, it is this very thing called "luck," whether it is good or bad, which goes to make the game what it is. And there are times, too, when bad luck strikes through no fault of your own, to leave a bitter taste in your mouth.

In 1919 I was working very hard to win the Tuna Club Red Button, awarded for taking a tuna of 50 pounds, or over, on regulation Light Tackle, i.e., a six-ounce tip and nine thread line. Since then the qualifying weight has been raised to 60 pounds, but at that time it was 50.

There were lots of fish ranging from 40 to 60 pounds. But somehow or other I simply couldn't get hold of one that would qualify me. Everything conceivable seemed to go wrong. I broke lines. I pulled out hooks. I missed strikes. If we went in one direction the fish showed up in another. Once my line actually came untied from the swivel. I was fishing with Smithy Warren and he took our luck as hardly as I did. Poor Old Smithy—he has gone down to the Happy Fishing Banks. I hope he has a party every day—and the best anglers in the game!

After nearly a month of disappointment we hooked a fish off the East End of Catalina that looked as though he would easily go 50 pounds. Everything went well for a change and we soon had him aboard. But once laid out on deck doubts began to assail us. Smithy thought he was all right—but, at the same time, shook his head and muttered that it didn't "look as though there were much margin." Certainly there was one thing we must do—get that fish weighed in as quickly as possible. It is surprising how much weight a fish loses after being caught—and how fast he loses it, too.

In this case we did everything proper to save weight. We plugged up the gaff hole, his mouth, his vent. We covered him with wet sacks which I kept soaked throughout our run back to Avalon. It seemed as though we would never get there. The *Fortuna* was slow, a scant six miles was her very best. As Smithy used to say, "She's so dad blamed slow she can't keep out o' her own shadder!"

At last we pulled up alongside the float at the end of Pleasure Pier. Tenderly we carried our prize up the gangway and laid it on the scales. Smithy wouldn't trust the official weigher to do the first weighing. He kneeled down and set the counter-weight at 50 pounds. It never even quivered! Swearing softly to himself he tapped it backward. At 49 pounds, 9 ounces it came into balance. Seven ounces short!

The next morning we were at it again. It was my last day. I simply had to go back to the mainland on the afternoon steamer. At eleven o'clock we hooked a fish. There was no doubt about this one. He would be a lot closer to 60 pounds than to 50. The kite broke away all right—or, at least, we thought it did.

I worked carefully on him until I had him within about thirty feet. Smithy was leaning over the side, peering down. Suddenly he straightened up and let out a stream of profanity such as I have never heard.

"That blankety blankety blanked kite line's all balled up down there!" he roared.

It was. Somewhere along the kite line there had been a weak spot. Instead of breaking off at the swivel it had broken close to the kite. The fish in his circling had whipped it around the line until it had formed a big wad three or four inches thick and a foot or more long. To make matters worse this wad was snarled about ten or fifteen feet above the swivel.

For half an hour we tried everything we could think of. The fish was practically dead, lying on his side, only his gills moving spasmodically. I brought the snarl up to the tip, but, of course, that was as far as it would go. Neither of us had a sharp knife, nor a pair of scissors. If we had had it would have been an easy matter to have cut the kite line free. A few snips and it would probably have dropped off. Smithy tried hacking at it with his dull jack-knife but with no results. He couldn't take hold of the fish line and try to unsnarl the tangle as that would disqualify the fish. I climbed up on top the *Fortuna's* cabin and held the rod high. But even then the swivel was at least three feet out of reach. At last we gave it up. Smithy wanted the fish anyhow, so, since it was dead, I told him to handline it in.

When we drew up at the Tuna Club float half a dozen old timers, seeing the fish on the stern and recognizing that it was a good sized one, and likewise knowing how hard I had been working for my button, came down to congratulate me.

I shall never forget Tom Manning, Secretary of the Club, after I had told my sad story.

"Damn the fishin' luck!" said he—and turned away.

[67]

The fish weighed 63 pounds. It was two years later before I won that coveted Red Button. Damn the fishin' luck!

Speaking of Red Buttons and Light Tackle, my mind goes back to the time when Jump took three bluefin tuna, in one week, on Light Tackle, and every one of them over 100 pounds—and when I ran his boat for him while he was doing it.

It started as a joke. Several years before he had performed the almost incredible feat of taking a 145-pound yellowfin tuna on regulation Light Tackle. Of course he was very proud of it—and justly so. And because he was so proud of it he had to stand a lot of ribbing about it. The fish was a yellowfin, and as such was not regarded as being in the same class with a bluefin. I don't know whether there is any difference in fighting qualities of the two fish or not. I have taken them both—and up to a hundred and forty or fifty pounds—and they both gave me plenty of argument. They put up such different types of fight, they take the bait so differently, they act so differently, that it is hard to compare them. Nevertheless the fact remains that, while no handicap in favor of the one as against the other is set up in the Tuna Club rules, there always has been a sort of feeling that a yellowfin is not the fish his cousin is.

Then Jim settled all argument—for a time, at least—by bringing in a 101-pound bluefin, the first one over 100 pounds ever taken on Light Tackle. But his triumph didn't last very long! One day Mrs. Keith Spalding came in with one weighing 103 pounds, and taken on Light Tackle. From then on, Jim's life was made miserable!

That particular year both Mankowski and Baker, two very fine Light Tackle experts, were fishing for hundred-pound bluefin on Light Tackle. Regarding that field of angling as more or less his own property Jump, deep in his heart, was, I think, a little resentful —and also worried.

At last, one night in the locker room, when the ribbing became a little too much for him, he lost his temper and challenged both Baker and Mankowski to beat him if they could. They jumped at it and a few bets were made.

Rob, Jump's son, who usually ran his boat for him, was ill, so he asked me if I would take his place.

"I can't let them two damn foreigners lick me!" he exclaimed— Baker was an Englishman and Mankowski was of Polish descent.

The first day out we landed a fine fish of 103 pounds. That was fine until a little later on in the day Mankowski came in with one of 105 pounds. Jump was wild!

The next morning we found tuna close in off the East End. There were lots of patches of floating kelp and the fish seemed to be hanging around them. The wind was just right and Jim dropped his bait neatly into a surfacing bunch. Instantly there was a smashing strike.

"*Got him!*" he yelled.

I had learned the day before something of what it was like to run a boat for him when hooked on to a big fish on Light Tackle. I can only say that it was no picnic and a vastly different matter than handling a boat with a tuna on Heavy Tackle. I had also noticed that a fish made an entirely different sort of fight. Instead of sounding, he kept on the surface, circling around us, for a long time. Nor did his first run seem as fast and furious as it is on Heavy Tackle. I couldn't figure that out, having always thought it must be just a matter of luck if one was able to stop the first run of a bluefin on Light Tackle. I did notice that Jim held his rod almost straight up, and high, and seemed to cover the reel with his hands. Later I learned the reason for the shortness of the first run and the subsequent circling, surface fight. As soon as the fish struck, Jump threw off all drag, merely thumbing the spool enough to prevent a backlash. With a small line, and no pressure, the fish had no incentive to rush headlong. It was more a case of swimming away. I have also learned since that the harder you fight them the harder they will fight back.

But to get back, as soon as the fish struck, I swung the *Ranger* after him. Soon he started to circle, just under the surface, fins and tail showing. I learned a lot about handling a boat that day. Jim was taking no chances on my inexperience. He told me what to do and I did it.

"Back up—Go ahead—Ahead six feet—Stop—Stop, I said!— Go astern—A little more—Stop the boat—Go to starboard a little —That's enough—Stop her—Straighten up—Port a little—That's enough—Stop her—Stop her, damn it!—Back up three feet—stop the boat—starboard a little—Hold her—Straighten up"—just a sample of the stream of orders that was fired at me. After forty-five minutes I was half-crazy and my arms ached from constant shoving in and out of the clutch lever. Jim didn't look too happy either. This fish was big and we knew it.

Presently he stopped circling and settled down. That made matters easier for me but not for Jump. The fish had to be pumped up. That is a hard enough job on Heavy Tackle. On Light it is twice as bad. A six-ounce tip and a nine thread line won't stand the punishment that a sixteen-ounce tip and twenty-four thread will. With the former it isn't main strength and awkwardness. It calls for finesse of the highest degree and never letting up the pressure for even a split second. But Jump was equal to the occasion. During the next twenty minutes I saw some of the finest angling that it has ever been my good fortune to see—skill, science, quick thinking to the ultimate degree, with never a false move, never too much, or too little pressure. I'll pay this compliment to Jimmie Jump. He is the greatest Light Tackle angler that ever lived. When that fish was alongside he hardly moved a fin. He was dead—killed on a six-ounce tip and a nine thread line that broke at 23 pounds!

Two hours later he weighed in at 113.5 pounds. That night we felt pretty good and didn't mind telling everybody so. But the next afternoon we didn't feel so good.

We had failed to find tuna and came in early. As we crossed the bay I saw a tuna flag flying from Smithy Warren's *Fortuna*. That meant he had a fish—Baker was fishing with him—and to be in that early that it was a pretty good one.

"Do you suppose that damned Englishman got a fish?" Jump growled, squinting at the flag.

Of course he had, or the flag wouldn't have been up. The question was how big was it? We soon found out—or thought we did.

As we passed the Tuna Club a whole crowd of fellows were out on the pier yelling at Jim. Finally, after someone had used a megaphone we learned the worst. Baker had brought in a fish weighing 122 pounds! Jim nearly had a stroke on the spot.

"You go ashore and find out if them birds are lyin'," he ordered as soon as we had made fast.

Once ashore plenty of kind hands led me to the bulletin board. There it was, for all to read. "Tuna—C. Alma Baker—122 pounds —Light Tackle." Well, that was a fine fish, and a splendid job on Baker's part. Then something about it struck me as being queer. All the boys were snickering. I looked at the legend again. There was something queer about that "122"! It looked as though the middle digit had been erased and the "2" written in. I began to smell a rat.

"What are you going to do with Jim?" someone asked.

"I haven't figured that out yet!" I answered. "Is this all on the level?"

Then they let me into the secret. Baker had brought in a fish, and a very fine one—112 pounds. Some joker had erased the "1" and substituted a "2," making it read "122." The whole idea was to have some fun with Jim—which was all right with me. The thing that had worried me the most was having to go out with him if Baker really had beaten him!

I rowed back to the *Ranger* and told him what I had seen, but not what I had heard. He took it pretty hard. As a matter of fact, he had been very proud of that hundred and thirteen pounder—as well he might be—and thought it would hang as a record for a long time. And now, the very next day, it was topped almost ten pounds. He puttered about the boat for a long time, obviously in no hurry to go ashore and take the jibes of the boys in the club. Anglers are a merciless gang!

When he did go ashore there was a reception committee waiting and they poured it on him pretty hard—too hard, I thought. As I have remarked, Jump was the greatest Light Tackle angler in the game. He, and he alone, had popularized that type of fishing. Even if he had lorded it over his class for years, nevertheless he earned every prize that came his way. And I will say this, too. He took his beating gamely—congratulating Baker on a fine fish and giving the others as good as he took.

After an hour or so of fun with him they confessed the joke. His face was a study. He blinked for a minute or two as though scarcely believing his ears, then laughed. But there wasn't much humor in that laugh. I don't think anyone ever did know quite how badly Jim had felt over those past few hours. It might be thought a sign of poor sportsmanship, but I can't agree. Light Tackle fishing was his child. He had talked it—had urged it—had proven that it could be done. He was head and shoulders above everyone else in that game. He took his fishing seriously. Judge him any way you please.

Next morning when I went aboard he said to me,

"Listen, kid, let's go out and fix these cusses once and for all. There's some big fish out there. Let's get ourselves one."

We got started early and headed out into the Clemente Channel. It looked as though we would have to connect that day or not at all. Tuna were getting scarce. It was not until we were off Silver Canyon that we saw a small bunch surfacing. They would show for a minute or two and then go down. When fish are acting that way they are hard to get. One must drop the bait into them just as they pop up. We were lucky. A small school surfaced just right for us and Jim skipped the bait smack into the middle of them.

They certainly boiled the water around that flying fish. It seemed as though every fish in the school was after it. One, however, and he looked big, leaped clear and smashed down upon it.

It was the same thing over again. No sooner had he hit than he started off, on the surface, and slowly, toward Clemente. After two or three hundred feet he turned in a big circle. Then followed forty minutes of the fastest work I have ever done, excepting, perhaps, that afternoon off the West End when Jump and I were among those great schools. For one thing we were both keyed up. The fish was big —bigger than anything we had taken so far. Jump wanted him badly. I, for my part, knew that if, through any mistake of my own in handling the boat, we should lose him I would never hear the end of it.

It was forty minutes before that fish sounded. When he did, Jim drew a deep breath.

"Now," he called out, "if we don't make some damn fool mistake we're going to get this bird!"

He pumped hard. There were times when I didn't see how that slender tip, that tiny line, could stand the strain. But they did. In about fifteen or twenty minutes I could see the shimmering blue-green of him deep down. Foot by foot Jump worked him up. Every second I expected the line to snap.

Just below the surface, the swivel wasn't more than a foot or six inches under water, the fish stuck and began to make little rushes back and forth. Things looked bad. Jim was tired. Light Tackle will stand just so much and no more. He was putting everything on it that it would stand and still the fish stuck. It was one of those times when one has to take a chance. Leaning far over the side I succeeded in getting hold of the leader just below the swivel. Then gently, very, very gently, I began to surge him upward. Two or three times I thought I would have to let go—but didn't. At last—and I think I must have held my breath that whole time—I had him up where I could make the gaff.

It was plain that he was a big fish. We measured him at 118 pounds. Two hours later he weighed in at 117.75, truly a remarkable fish to be taken on Light Tackle. It may be argued that there was but five pounds difference between this one and Baker's fish. True enough—but I have found this. When a tuna tops 115 pounds he appears to take on harder fighting qualities than those which are under that weight. I don't know why—but I have found it so, at least. Anyhow he was a Tuna Club record, probably a Light Tackle world record at the time—and is a Tuna Club record today. As a matter of fact I don't know that anyone has taken a larger bluefin on regulation Light Tackle anywhere—but perhaps they have. I don't know.

BIG TUNA

AND still we are on the subject of tuna. But this time it is *Big Tuna!*

There are big fish in the sea. Any big game angler will agree to that. Zane Grey once remarked to the effect that there was never an angler lived but that there was a fish capable of taking the conceit out of him! Truer words were never spoken.

And it is the *big* fish that generally get away. Why shouldn't they? To attain great size in the face of that furious, merciless struggle for existence which forever rages under the face of the sea a fish must develop qualities which set him apart from his kind—just as must a man who, in the face of stern competition, reaches the top of the ladder. And these qualities must, of necessity, be strength, stamina and cunning.

There are big tuna in various parts of the world. And, while the tuna about which Catalina fishing has grown are small compared to those of the North Atlantic and the North Sea, nevertheless in the Southern California channels, as well as elsewhere, are very, very big tuna. A few of us have had the good fortune to get into these huge fish and have returned sadder and wiser by reason of our experience.

One evening a Slavonian market fisherman approached me in a state of great excitement. From the torrent of broken English I gathered that he had been albacore fishing off the West End of San Clemente Island and had there encountered enormous tuna. They must have been big. Fish are just fish to commercial fishermen. It takes very large ones, and lots of them, to start them raving. He was

[77]

a little vague about exact locations, but, as near as I could understand, they were somewhere about half way between San Clemente and Santa Barbara Islands—a considerable area of water.

The next morning Captain Roy and I were off after them. For two days we cruised up and down and back and forth, lying in at night in the Goose Neck of Clemente. There were signs of fish—lots of them. Birds squatting on the surface. Scales, tiny whirlpools, that fishy look to the sea which is so unmistakable, and so impossible to describe. But not a fish did we see other than an occasional shark.

The third morning we held a council of war. Roy was deep in the dumps.

"Here's how things stand," he explained. "We got just 'nuff gas for today an' to git us home. I dunno what yuh got in mind but how's this strike yuh? S'pose we take a long reach up toward Santa Barb'ra. Then, if we don't find nothin' we kin run back to Av'lon 'round th' north side th' island. Then, if we should find ourselves gittin' low on gas there's always boats layin' in them coves up 'round th' Isthmus. We could borry some off somebody. That sound O.K. by you?"

I couldn't see that we had much choice in the matter. It was disappointing to have to leave such abundant signs of fish. But it would be a lot worse to run out of gas in those lonely waters.

That last day promised to be perfect. The fog broke early, melted away by the sun rather than blown away by the wind. The breeze was light, but enough for a kite. The northwest roll was gentle.

We worked up to westward. There was still some bird life hanging around but not nearly so much as the other days. Nor did the sea have the appearance of fish that it had had. The further we went the more empty it seemed to grow. There were a few shearwaters, a few terns, a few high flying gulls, and that was all.

[78]

BIG TUNA

By noon I had given up—but not Roy. He was perched on top the cabin, ever alert, ever on watch. Twice he called down that he thought he saw splashes far ahead. But they didn't materialize into fish.

When we ate lunch I suggested that we might as well call quits.

"Not yet a while," he answered. "There ain't no hurry. I just measured th' gas an' we got 'nuff to go a piece further an' still leave 'nuff to git home on an' to spare. Yuh never can tell when somethin's liable to happen. This here water looks good to me."

It didn't to me, but I knew better than to argue. If I had insisted on starting home then and there, for years on end Roy would have kept on reminding me that, if we had only gone on a "piece further" we would have found the fish.

I think it was about half-past one, and I was half asleep, when there was a thump in the cockpit and Roy was shaking me awake.

"For cripe's sake! For cripe's sake! Lookit! Lookit!" he kept shouting and pointing ahead. I jumped up and looked.

There, not a half mile ahead, the whole ocean seemed to be a turmoil of boiling water, it was almost like a wall of white water rushing down upon us. Out of that wall, out of that broken turmoil, huge black shapes lunged and leaped. Ahead of them, spreading out fan-wise, frantic, like silver rain came the bait—sardines, flying fish, anchovies, mackerel. And, down the air lanes, racing to the kill, came birds—myriads of birds, apparently coming up out of empty space. It was a sight, once seen never to be forgotten. I had seen hungry feeding tuna before. But never, never had I seen anything to equal this. Those fish were simply unbelievable! It seemed utterly impossible that there could be fish so huge, so furious in their leaps, or so many of them. I had always held to the belief that large fish were only found in small schools—and here, before my very eyes, the ocean, as far as I could see, was literally alive with them!

I think both of us went a little crazy for a minute or two. Roy jumped around the cockpit, clapping his hands and shouting,

"What'd I tell yuh! What'd I tell yuh!"

I don't know what I did. Roy said afterward that I just stood there, fumbling with the rod, staring stupidly at those onrushing fish.

In less time than the telling takes they were upon us. The noise was terrific! "SWISSSSSSH! SWISSSSSSSH! SWISSSSSSH!" of sharp fins cutting the surface. "CRAAAAAASH! CRAAAAAASH! CRAAAAAASH!" as great bronze shapes lunged clear and smashed back. And, overhead, a bedlam of screaming, fighting seabirds.

My bait lagged sluggishly. A puff of wind caught the kite and jerked up and forward. The bait leaped into the air and smashed back.

"SWISSSSSH! CRAAAAASH! CRAAAAASH! CRAAAASH!" The water seemed to explode. Half a dozen fish lunged at once. One, and what a fish he was, leaped clear and crashed squarely down upon it. I'll swear that white water threw six feet into the air. The rod was almost jerked from my grasp!

"*Strike! Strike!*"

"RRRRRREEEEEEEEEEEEEEEEEEEEEEEEEEEEE!"

The reel didn't snarl—it screamed. Line melted off as though blown away.

"*Snap!*"

The line went limp. The tip jerked up. Broken off!

Roy snorted disgustedly as he dove into the bait box for another flying fish.

[80]

"What th' hell happened?" he demanded. "Why didn't yuh let 'im go?"

It struck me that that was precisely what I had done—but I didn't answer. The kite had gone—neither of us even saw it fall. He tossed up another on a very short line—just enough to let it fly and drag the bait.

The flying fish wasn't twenty feet from the side when—

"WHISSSSSH! CRAAAASH! RRRRREEEEEE! SNAP!"

Another big fellow nailed it, was off like an express train, and snapped the line. Two gone—both broken off. Roy went berserk. He shook his fist at the leaping fish all around us. He kicked the bait box. He cursed savagely. He shook his fist in my face.

"What th' hell's th' matter with you?" he roared. "Didn't yuh never catch a fish before? For Christ's sake let 'em go!"

He quieted down and spat overside. Then, patiently, speaking slowly, as though instructing a child, he went on.

"Now lissen! We've spent three whole days runnin' 'round this here ocean lookin' for these here fish. Now that we've found 'em, you go ahead an' lose 'em fast as we hook 'em! That ain't no sense. Yuh gotta take th' drag off soon as they hit! Can't yuh understand?"

I tried to explain that I *had* thrown all the drag off—letting the line run free. But he shook his head.

"That's what *you* think!" he retorted. "You're excited an' dunno what you're doin'. Now just settle down on th' next one just like he was nothin' but an ordinary hundred pounder. GOOD GOD ALMIGHTY!"

His jaw dropped—and I guess mine did, too. Not fifty feet from the boat a tuna came out of the water—and what a tuna! Four times he jumped clear in great twisting jumps that took him fifteen feet into the air. Jumps that showed us his depth, the breadth of his shoulders, his length. If that fish was an inch he was all of fifteen feet long. Remember now, he wasn't fifty feet away from us. I had seen some pretty big fish in my time—and have seen some big ones since. But never before or since have I seen his equal. I wouldn't even guess what he weighed, but, allowing for excitement, for amazement, I still think he could have gone anywhere between fifteen hundred and two thousand pounds.

Roy's reaction was comical. He stared at the spreading green swirl, then took off his hat and swept the deck with it.

"Ex—*cuse me*, mister! If *that*'s a sample of what you've had aholt of I ain't got nuthin' more to say!"

After that huge creature leaped out we stopped for a few minutes and watched the marvelous sight of those great fish. They seemed to be everywhere—as far as we could see. While I don't know, I doubt that there was one vast school of them. Rather, I would think, there were innumerable small schools, but so many of them, and so close together, that they gave the impression of one great body of milling, feeding fish. As I watched them lunge out, their backs, broad as a rowboat tearing along the surface, their incredible speed, the fury of their onslaught upon the helpless bait, their great, twisting leaps, I was filled with a sense of the utter futility of trying to stop, let alone land, one.

But hope springs eternal in the angler's breast. Something might happen, luck might perch upon our shoulders, we even might get hold of a sick one! Roy threw up another kite and I let the bait out.

"SWISSSSSH. CRAAAAASH! RRRRREEEEEE! SNAP!"

The same story over again. A furious, smashing strike—the scream of the reel—the snap of a broken line. And so it went for over three hours. I lost all count of time and of happenings. I caught myself muttering some silly sort of prayer that I might stop one of these great fish—just one. As though the Force that rules all things should show *me* any favor—should graciously permit me to take a life that was just as precious to its possessor as mine was to me. How impertinent we mortals are!

We had a dozen and a half baits. Most of them were lost on good clean strikes and broken lines. Three or four times, however, so many fish hit at once that the bait was crushed to a pulp. At last I was aware of a tap on the shoulder. I looked up. There was Roy. There was a dry grin on his face and he held up a single flying fish.

"Here she is, mister!" he announced. "She's th' last one! Better spit on her fer luck. When she's gone we'll git goin' too."

I did spit on it—something I don't think I ever did before or since—and tossed it overside. The kite pulled it away, wriggling, dragging over the surface.

"SWISSSSSH. CRAAAAASH! RRRRRREEEE! SNAP!"

And that was that. We stared hopelessly at one another. Roy shook his head and spat.

"It just can't be done!" he muttered, and threw in the clutch, came about and headed back toward Catalina. It was a long, gloomy trip, that forty-mile traverse back to Avalon.

Since then I have been in those same fish twice. Other anglers have been in them as well. Always the story is the same. A strike, a headlong, furious rush, a broken line. In my three experiences with them I don't think I ever saw a fish that weighed less than four hundred pounds.

I think Roy was right. I don't think "it can be done"! Not out here in the Pacific, at least. I doubt that the man is born or the tackle made capable of stopping and landing one of those giant Pacific bluefin tuna. I make this statement with full knowledge of the astoundingly large fish that have been taken in Nova Scotia, Maine and the North Sea. I know one man, Stapleton-Cotton, of the British Tunny Club, who took six tunny, averaging over six hundred pounds each, *in one day!* Grey, Farrington, Mrs. Farrington, Peel, dozens of others have taken great tuna. How they do it, I don't know—unless there is a difference between our big tuna out here and those of the Atlantic and the North Sea.

I have tried to figure it out. I believe the anglers of the Catalina Tuna Club are as capable as others elsewhere in the world. I don't think they are any better, but *are* just as good. And yet there has never been a one of us who has had the experience of getting into those big fish but has come home beaten and humiliated. I have only one explanation.

Out here our waters are very deep, two, three, four thousand feet. To get a strike out of a bluefin tuna we must use a kite bait. We have guessed and experimented until we have come to the conclusion that an ordinary hundred-pound tuna as it hits such a bait gets up a speed of nearly fifty miles an hour. How fast a thousand pounder is going, God knows! The fish comes out of the water and lunges down upon the bait. He never stops. No sooner does he feel the hook than he plunges downward—with three thousand feet of water beneath him. That downward rush, the drag of the line through the water, is just too much for tackle to stand.

Where big tuna are successfully taken on rod and reel conditions are different. The waters are comparatively shoal. I am told by those who have taken them that the fish make more of a surface fight—heavy, sullen, and not unlike that of a broadbill. If this is true I can understand how it is possible to get very large fish. You give me a fish that stays on the surface, and doesn't take off for China at the speed of a streamlined train, and I will show you one that can be caught. Sooner or later you are going to get close enough to him to get a gaff home.

Then, too, there is the matter of tackle—an exceedingly delicate subject. The maximum heavy tackle under Tuna Club regulations consists of a sixteen-ounce tip and twenty-four thread line, the latter with a maximum breaking strain, when dry, of sixty-six pounds. That classification of tackle has appeared to be adequate for our normal requirements over a period of forty years. And that is the tackle which most of us who have been in these big fish have used. Perhaps that is why we don't even stop them. On the other hand I know of two cases where the angler used thirty-nine thread line and it broke just as quickly as did twenty-four. Furthermore there have been some pretty good sized fish taken on Tuna Club regulation heavy tackle—broadbill up to nearly six hundred pounds and marlin to nearly seven hundred. Not that broadbill and marlin fight the same sort of fight as do tuna. But a marlin, especially, is a pretty fast fish. He is on the surface, out of the water, deep down, everywhere. It is a good angler who can keep a constant tight line on one. And, too, it must be admitted that any game fish that tops five hundred pounds is far from being a soft touch for anybody!

In examining the records of big tuna taken in other places I find that lines range from thirty-nine to seventy-two, with forty-five and fifty-four most commonly used. I also understand that they are fished for from rowboats, still fishing. That would seem to me to be of great advantage to the angler. The bait being stationary the fish takes it slowly. There is every possibility of the fish swallowing the bait and hooking himself deep in his throat, even his stomach. Then, too, with a heavy line a rowboat can be towed—I don't say they are, but they can be. When the fish becomes exhausted the boat can be pulled over to the fish, the fish pulled to the boat. To my mind that would be a great advantage after a long fight.

Let me make myself quite clear. I have no fault to find with any tackle that any angler cares to use. That is his affair. Differing conditions call for different tackle regulations. I do wish, though, that some enterprising angler would try those big tuna of Atlantic and North Sea waters on Tuna Club regulation heavy tackle. I also wish that it might happen that someone, using extra heavy tackle, might get into those very large bluefin tuna which sometimes visit the Southern California island channels. It would be interesting to see what happened. Until someone proves me wrong, however, I am standing firm on Captain Roy's axiom.

"It just can't be done!"

I came close to proving myself wrong once.

Tuna were scarce. Scarce, that is for all but Boschen. Day after day the rest of us chased the channels fruitlessly. Day after day Boschen and Farnsworth came in with fish, all of good size. No one knew where they were finding them—and they didn't tell. There was a good deal of grousing about it but I don't know that I blame them. After all, if Farnsworth took enough interest in the game to spend years in study and observation, if he was ambitious enough to sit up nights checking and cross-checking his data to the end that he might find fish when fish were not, then why should he broadcast his findings. Fishing was his living. We all of us, boatmen and anglers, had the same opportunities for study and knowledge that he had.

About the only thing upon which we were agreed was that the fish were probably somewhere out in the Clemente Channel. But that didn't help much. It is a pretty sizable body of water, that channel. The *Mabel F* was faster than the rest of the Avalon boats of that time. Many tried to follow her but Farnsworth seemed to take delight in losing them—and coming back with fish that night.

One evening my boatman, Enos Vera, an Azores Portuguese with an uncanny fishing sense inherited from generations of fishing ancestors, said that he thought these tuna were somewhere off the West End of Clemente. Instead of trying to follow Boschen and Farnsworth, which, in the little *Pirate* would be a hopeless task, he suggested that we start early and lie in wait for them off Salto Verde Point. It was just possible that we might obtain a hint as to their course from that point.

The morning was overcast and somewhat thick. Visibility was poor—not more than a mile at the most. Off Catalina's East End the weather was cold and raw, the sea grey and empty appearing. There were a few cruising birds, an occasional patch of bait. What wind there was was southerly. The only boat in sight was a lone grouper fisherman bobbing up and down about a mile and a half off Seal Rocks. We followed the coast of the island and about two miles offshore, just loafing along.

Two hours passed. Once we saw a market fisherman on the horizon—and later a boat passed us inshore. In the haze we couldn't make her out properly, but she looked like the *Mabel F.* If she were, we were on about the same course.

Once clear of Salto Verde Point we kept on going into the haze on a course that would ultimately take us about six miles off the West End of San Clemente. Suddenly Enos stiffened.

"Lotta birds ahead," he announced, pointing.

The sea seemed to be alive with them, milling and swooping—and, to send us both tumbling off the cabin in a hurry, beneath them appeared big splashes and dark, boiling swirls. Feeding tuna!

Everything was just right. The kite was up and a bait out. The wind was in the right direction to put us properly into the fish. We were alone. There were no other boats to come racing up and possibly drive the fish down.

As we drew nearer we drove scolding sea birds from under our bows—birds so stuffed with food that they could hardly fly. I jerked the rod. The bait leaped into the air and splashed back close to those spreading swells. I jerked again—and again it leaped ahead. Enos yelled. For an instant it lagged as the kite met a soft spot. It seemed to me I saw a shadow beneath it. Then it skittered and jumped. The water parted. A broad, bronze back lunged furiously at it. We both shouted at the size of him. He seemed so big and heavy that he had difficulty coming out, seeming rather to hump himself after the skittering bait than to make the usual clean leap of a striking tuna. I jerked the bait, and he was after it again. Two thirds of him must have come out, and again we shouted as we realized the width, the depth, the length of him. Down he crashed squarely upon the skittering bait. White water boiled and flew. A great green swirl eddied and spread. The rod was almost jerked out of my hands. The kite line snapped and the kite fluttered down.

"*Strike! Strike! Strike!*" I yelled—and struck him. It was like surging back against a rock!

The reel screamed—it didn't snarl. The reel itself grew hot to the touch. Enos had gone into reverse and we were grinding astern, as we sought to ease the strain and slow that furious run.

[88]

"RRRRREEEEEEE-E-E-E-RRRRRRRRRRRRRRR!!"
The scream deepened to a throaty snarl. The run slackened, picked
up again, again slackened, then slowed and finally stopped. Enos ran
aft and seized me by the shoulders, shaking me.

"You be careful, please!" he cried. "Oh-oh—you be careful!
Don' you make-a no meestak now! *She mos' beeg tunny I ever see!*"

There was no doubt about it being big. My first heave on him
told me that. It was as though I were hooked to kelp, to a rock!
Then, after a few sullen surges, he commenced to circle and bore.
I seemed to be in a dream. It didn't seem possible that his rush had
been stopped and that he had settled down to the typical tuna fashion
of fighting. I had had a good look at the fish when he struck. I
didn't think he was anywhere near as big as those great fish I had
met off the West End of San Clemente, but he was big enough,
nearly as large as the 251-pound Tuna Club record, perhaps larger.
With any kind of luck we should get him. It was only about nine in
the morning. The sea was smooth and promised to remain that way
for hours to come. Everything was in our favor. I slipped out of my
sweater and went to work.

I pumped hard, but carefully, satisfied to get a few inches of line
at a time. For about half an hour we had it back and forth. Sometimes I would get quite a bit of line piled back, then it would be
ripped off again. But, taking it by and large, I was gaining slowly,
but surely. Somehow or other, perhaps because his run *had* been
stopped, I had a feeling that I was going to get him. I started to lift.

"*Snap!*" I nearly fell backward out of the chair. The rod jerked
up—the line went limp. He was gone. For a minute or two Enos was
speechless, staring at me with open mouth. Then he struck one hand
against the other.

[89]

"Oh-Oh-Oh! What you do!" he demanded, almost on the verge of tears. "Don' tell me you lose that tunny! Why don' you be careful like I say?"

Well, I had lost "that tunny" all right, but how I had managed to lose him I didn't know, until I reeled in the line. Then the story was clear to read. The double line was severed as cleanly as though cut with a knife. Undoubtedly this was what had happened. Of course the line was very tight. The fish had rushed back into the school from which he had been hooked—or another school had gathered around him. One of two things had then occurred: Either another fish had brushed against the tight line with his fins, or had snapped at the air bubbles racing up from the swivel.

Both of us, but Enos particularly, were crushed. Mechanically we straightened things up, rigged a new bait and leader, then looked about us. With that our spirits rose again. Everywhere were tuna—big tuna—rolling and surfacing. Another boat had come up out of nowhere, Shorty Stoughton. A bare hundred yards from us they had a smashing strike. Their kite didn't break off and the fish jerked it under. I remember seeing the sticks fly as it struck the surface. Half a dozen big fish boiled up within twenty feet of our boat. I thought we would never get going again. The first kite Enos threw up wouldn't fly and before he got through fooling with it he was all tangled up in the line. The next one was bridled improperly and shot off to one side. More precious minutes lost! But the third one caught a puff of wind, just at the right moment, and sailed off and upward. But our troubles weren't over yet. There were tuna everywhere—but for some reason we couldn't get into them, couldn't get a rise. Back and forth we cruised, bait and kite working perfectly, but with not the sign of a strike. The other boat had landed their fish—or lost it—and were hooked on to another. My mind persistently dwelt upon the one we had lost. How big was he? What could I have done to save him? I had a sense that our big chance had been given us and we had missed.

"*Look out!*" This from Enos.

A swift shadow darted under the bait. I jerked the rod. The flying fish started to jump ahead and the water parted and out came a tuna to nail it hard.

"*Strike! Strike!*" I yelled, at the same time hitting him—but without any enthusiasm. The fish was small—not over sixty or seventy pounds.

"Hurry up!" Enos called. "You get 'im quick! He jus' litty bitty tunny! That jus' our luck!"

I thought so too, but somehow or other it didn't look as though I was going to "get 'im quick." He made a terrific run, then settled down to a stubborn, lugging fight. Around and around he circled, boring downward, jabbing and jerking. Before long I realized that, "litty bitty" or not, I was in for all the tussle I wanted. Enos wasn't helping matters any by perpetually nagging at me to hurry up.

Inch by inch and foot by foot, every inch and every foot stubbornly contested, I was gaining on him, but never once did he quit— never for an instant did I dare let up on him.

At last the hundred-foot marker came out and spooled onto the reel. Enos was hanging over the side peering down into the water.

"I see 'im! I see 'im!" he shouted. "He hunder pounder all right!"

I pumped the swivel out and swung it toward him. He grabbed it, then began to reach aimlessly with his other hand. The fish was surging heavily.

[91]

"Where my gaff?" he cried. "Gimme my gaff! Hurry up! I no can hold 'im!"

I looked and there it was, clear up forward. By the time I had gotten it (the point was stuck into the rail) and handed it to him, he had had to let the fish go. I could have murdered him then and there!

That fish had had a breathing space while I was scrambling for the gaff. When Enos let him go he ripped off about three hundred feet and stuck there, evidently having been as close to the boat as he ever wanted to be again. I worked hard for one solid hour before I was able to bring the swivel to Enos' hand again.

Once lashed down on the stern the fish looked big—a lot bigger than he had appeared when he struck. Enos thought he would go one hundred and ten pounds—later he added another ten—and I guessed him at about ninety to a hundred.

Three hours later he weighed in at 149 pounds and turned out to be the season's record!

Now, your guess is as good as mine. We had hooked a fish we knew was very large and had lost him. A little later we hooked another that undoubtedly weighed at the time more than 150 pounds and he appeared so small in comparison to the first one that we both thought him not more than a sixty pounder. How big was that other —the one we lost? No four or five hundred pounder, I know, but if he didn't beat three hundred, I never saw a big fish in my life!

MARLIN SMASHING BACK

OUT OF THE DEPTHS

THE following is set down somewhat hesitantly. He who ventures aside from the accepted grooves of belief lays himself open not alone to jibes, but to direct attack upon his veracity. It is human nature to scoff at those things which are not understood, or which are not simple of explanation. The most startling incident related in the following pages I experienced myself, saw with my own eyes. Some twenty-five or thirty personal acquaintances, all of them reputable, many of them men of substance and standing in their respective communities, also saw with their own eyes the identical thing which I saw. The reader is at liberty to believe, or not to believe, what follows. However the fact remains that it happened; that I saw what I am about to describe.

It was in September of the year 1916. I was over at San Clemente Island after marlin swordfish. We left Mosquito Harbor about seven o'clock in the morning. The day was overcast with high fog, and windless. The sea was like glass except for a small roll coming down the coast. All objects on the surface, birds and driftwood, appeared black. Visibility was perfect, the sea stretching away to the sharp line of the horizon. These details are important, so bear them in mind.

By about eight o'clock we were perhaps a mile and a half off White Rock which is some three miles above Mosquito. I was sitting on top of the cabin watching for fins, my field glasses beside me. My boatman was busy at something down in the cockpit. A bait was out and the rod lashed to the fishing chair.

Suddenly, out of the corner of my eye, and to seaward, I saw something big and black lifting above the surface. I whirled, gasped, then clapped my glasses on it and yelled to my boatman to head for it. A scant quarter of a mile off there reared up out of the water the Thing which I instinctively knew was what, for years, we had called the "Clemente Monster," which many had seen, and about which there had been endless wonderment. I shall try to describe it to you as best I can.

Try to imagine a great columnar neck, or body, eight to ten feet thick and lifting twenty feet above the surface. Surmount this neck or body with a flat-topped, blunt, reptilian head. On either side of the head place two huge, round and bulging eyes. I don't believe they were an inch under a foot and a half across, perhaps more. There you have the essentials of what we saw.

At my first shout my boatman stuck his head out of the cabin jitney and let out a queer little squawk. I don't know that I blame him particularly!

Steadily we forged toward the Thing. Remember, it was about a quarter of a mile away. My glasses were of seven power. I had them on it from the first moment I caught a glimpse of it. I don't know precisely, but would guess that they brought it up to within a couple of hundred yards of us. Certainly I could see it plainly enough to note various details.

Two things stood out above all others—those enormous eyes and its unbelievably huge bulk. I never want to look at such eyes again. They were like the creations of a nightmare! Their very size, of course, left one breathless. But that was only a detail. It is utterly impossible to describe the coldness, the expressionlessness of them. It was like looking into the dim past when earth's life consisted of great, slimy, horrible creatures dragging their way through gargantuan forests and over dead, sullen seas. They literally froze me in my seat. Later my man said that I was as white as a sheet, my teeth chattering, my knees shaking. I wouldn't be surprised. Neither in a museum, nor in any reconstructed picture of a prehistoric creature have I ever seen eyes which resembled those.

The trunk, or neck, or whatever it was that appeared above the surface, seemed to be covered with coarse, reddish-brown bristles. It wasn't hair. They stood out rigidly from the body. It is strange that I should have gathered any impression of color in that light, but I did and, as will develop later, it is quite likely that I was correct in my impression.

The trunk, or neck, was more or less erect. The head was turning slowly as though surveying the surface of the sea. The Thing did not rise and fall in the slight roll of the sea. Instead the waves *broke against it*. Give full consideration to what that statement means!

I gathered the impression that the head was lowered. Certainly I saw nothing resembling a mouth. Others who have seen it say they saw a mouth. I didn't.

The great head continued its pivoting, seeming to make three-quarters of a circle. Then it saw us. The pivoting stopped. Those terrible eyes fixed themselves upon us coldly and without any expression noticeable through the lenses of the field glasses. For a few moments it regarded us fixedly, then, as though some great, hidden hand had seized it, it slowly sank. There was no visible movement of the great trunk, no commotion on the surface. Slowly, majestically, by comparison making the fluking of a whale seem a panicky, convulsive dive, it sank and disappeared beneath the surface. There was no swirl, no bubbles to mark where it had been, or where it sank.

I don't know how long it was up; perhaps a minute and a half,

[95]

perhaps two. My boatman claims five or ten, but that is ridiculous. Our boat being slow, by the time we had turned toward it I doubt that we approached appreciably closer. So, what I saw I saw from about a quarter of a mile away and through the lenses of field glasses.

Such an experience as I had comes only to a fortunate few. Coming face to face with an impossible creature, something unknown, something that cannot be, rocks one's powers of judgment and observation. I have no doubt at all but that there were many interesting details which I missed entirely. I am not at all surprised that such should be the case. If I had not known at the first glimpse what it was that I saw; if I had not heard about it before, heard it described; if I had not caught a distant glimpse of it some time before, I doubt that I would have been able to observe as much detail as I did.

This former glimpse didn't amount to much. I was tuna fishing in the Clemente Channel. It was very rough; big, combing seas. About a mile away something big, black and shiny lifted against the horizon. Then a series of breaking seas hid it and I saw it no more. But it was enough to tell me that the tales which had been brought in about something strange and large out in that channel had a foundation in fact. Subsequently, after the close-up view of it just related, I saw it again, but again a long way off and with just a momentary glimpse.

It is a little difficult to describe my emotions after the Thing sank. I had always loved the sea, particularly around and about San Clemente Island. With the appearance of that Thing, and its disappearance beneath the waters across which we were fishing, something of the friendliness went out of that sea and didn't come back for a long time. I caught myself glancing furtively overside and with a strange prickling sensation up and down my spine. We went on fishing that day but neither of us was particularly happy. I know I felt a pronounced sense of relief when we dropped our hook in Mosquito that night and I stepped out upon the security of land—and that in the face of the jibes of my fellow anglers when I told my story.

I have said that others have seen the Thing. With the exception that some claim to have seen a mouth, descriptions tally almost to the dot. There is also, of course, some divergence of description as to the height the creature rears up. This ranges from ten to thirty feet. But I think that is understandable and explainable. It is doubtful that, in each appearance, it lifts to exactly the same height. I may be mistaken in my estimate—anyone can be. However, I am a moderately good judge of distance, horizontal and vertical, and I am of the firm belief that the Thing, when I saw it, lifted up a good twenty feet.

There was nothing serpentine about it, except, perhaps, the head. The impression I gathered was of a huge neck which must have led to an unbelievably huge body. But more of that later.

The Thing has been reported all along the Pacific Coast from Monterey to Ensenada, although it has been seen most often in the San Clemente Channel and fairly close to the island. I am satisfied there is more than one. I don't believe one individual roams that length of coastline. I do not think that it necessarily lives at any great depth. I feel certain that it is a mammal and must come up to breathe. Neither I, nor anyone else, has seen any signs of gills, or even gill slits. It could come up a dozen times a day, even oftener, and, unless a boat happened to be right there, it could easily miss being seen.

So far as I know there have been three other men closer to the Thing than I was. Two of these had an extraordinary experience. They were near San Clemente with the engine shut down while they ate lunch. Suddenly the Thing came out within two hundred feet of them. Both knew what it was and kept very still. It watched them for some minutes, its head pivoting, its great eyes fixed upon them, then went down only to come up again in a few minutes at a different spot. This kept up for half an hour. It would come up, look them over, go down, then come up again. Obviously it was curious about them, but made no move toward coming closer. One of these men thinks that some years later he caught a glimpse of the Thing beneath his boat. He happened to look overside and was startled to see a great, reddish-brown mass lunging forward about thirty feet beneath him. He had just a flash of it, saw neither beginning nor end, and it was gone. It was of enormous size, he said, and far larger than any whale. As a matter of fact, a whale, thirty feet down, doesn't appear anywhere near his actual size.

Well, there it is. You now know as much about it as I do. I don't think there is the shadow of a doubt but that, here in our Southern California channels, and to northward, there exists an unknown species of great sea creature—perhaps come down to us out of the prehistoric past. I have further corroborative evidence, other than that of those who have seen the Thing, to support me in this. About seven years ago a Los Angeles man, interested in scientific research and possessed of a yacht to take him to out-of-the-way places, was at anchor in Acapulco Bay. One day he took the launch and went down the coast a way, beaching her and going ashore at an inlet. In walking down the beach he came to great, three-toed tracks leading up out of the sea and across the *wet* sand. There was a mark between, like a furrow, that might have been caused by the drag of a tail. He found where the creature had rolled and wallowed in the warm sand, the barrel-like depression made by its body, and its track back to the sea. All this, mind you, must have happened between the tides. He measured the tracks as best he could and estimated that they were fully *three feet long and over two feet across*. This man was thoroughly reliable, of high standing, and of a scientific turn of mind.

When I was a little boy two wide-eyed Mexicans came into Los Angeles with an astounding tale. Hunting rabbits in the sand dunes between what is now Huntington Beach and Newport Bay they had come across three-toed tracks, with a furrow between them, leading up out of the surf and across the beach. Following them they came to signs of where the creature had rolled in the sand. They became very frightened and ran away. They swore, however, that the tracks were "almost two paces long"! It is strange how the two reports, forty years apart and from points fifteen hundred miles distant from one another, dovetail!

I can't help it if the men of science do say there can be no such thing. I know better, for I have seen it. How can we know what is in the sea? As long as men have sailed ships they have brought in tales of sea serpents. Not all of them have been liars. Very recently, in the magazines *London Illustrated News* and *Life* appeared photographs of the long reported Lake Okonogon "monster." Okonogon is a long lake extending from British Columbia into our state of Washington. For years there have been tales told of something strange inhabiting it. Now a picture has been published of this thing and I assume that it is authentic. It shows, about three hundred feet from shore, a serpentine creature apparently about seventy-five feet long. The undulations of its barrel-like body are plain to see. Under a strong glass the head appears to be blunt and reptilian. One tail lobe appears above the surface. Then there is the Loch Ness "monster." Many reputable people of every walk of life claim to have seen it. Again, we have the twin "monsters" which made frequent appearances off the Straits of Juan de Fuca, leading into Puget Sound.

Entirely aside from anything I may have seen, I can't understand why anyone, scientist or otherwise, should dogmatically declare that such things are impossible—especially in the sea. We know that great monsters once lived on land. Changing environment drove them into extinction. We also know that great monsters inhabited the sea. There environment has not changed so greatly as it has on land. Three-quarters of the earth's surface is covered by sea. The greatest depths are over a mile deeper than the greatest heights are high— although, in so far as these creatures are concerned, I don't think depth has anything to do with the matter. Why, then, say that such creatures are impossible? One thing is certain—they can't be seen from a den, a library, or a laboratory.

In any event I did see something strange and terrible. I can only wish that any skeptics might have been with me that September morning off Clemente and seen that Thing lifting above the surface, looked into those great eyes!

The sea is a strange place—smiling, friendly, sometimes, and yet, at the same time, unutterably lonely. Knocking about its surface in small boats one sees and hears things that can't be explained.

I think I am a moderately well balanced individual, and yet I have heard voices at sea at night just as plainly as I have heard them in a room—only I didn't know what they were saying. Of course imagination plays strange tricks. At night, alone upon the immensity of the sea, one might imagine one heard almost anything. Metaphysicians say that thoughts are things. If they are, that would account for many otherwise unaccountable experiences people have had.

OUT OF THE DEPTHS

One strange experience, not of hearing but of seeing, and at night, remains very vividly with me. I was lost in a pea soup fog in the Catalina Channel. I shouldn't have been lost, but I was. Night shut down. We knew in a general way where the island lay but we had not the slightest idea at which end of it we were. We were anxious to make Avalon. On the other hand, being in a sailing boat it didn't seem wise to go barging headlong through the fog toward the island. It seemed the better part of wisdom to feel our way cautiously until the fog lifted enough to permit us to learn where we were. Of course we kept a couple of men up forward as lookouts.

Along about eleven o'clock they let out a yell that they could see the lights of Avalon. Sure enough, dead ahead (and that surprised me because I thought we were paralleling the island) could be seen a considerable luminosity, very much as would be made by a great number of electric lights shining through fog.

Straight for this glow we headed, satisfied that our aimless wanderings were ended and that we had made port.

We entered that luminosity and sailed right through it into darkness again!

What was it? I don't know.

Speaking of strange sounds at night, some of the most common manifestations are bells ringing, and wailing voices. These might be anything—imagination and lonesomeness probably. However I have heard locomotives whistling sixty or seventy miles offshore. Probably due to some abnormal conductivity of air currents—nevertheless that is a long way to hear them.

I was fishing on and off from Long Point, Catalina, late one afternoon. Big tuna had been seen there and we were having a try at

[101]

them. Back and forth we worked, trolling a kite bait. There was a stiff westerly blowing and it was hard to keep the bait in the water. The sun dropped behind the island and dusk began to settle. We reached in from some six or seven miles and then came about somewhere around a mile and a half offshore for one final tack seaward before giving it up as a bad job and going home. As we turned I just happened to glance overside and saw, not fifteen feet beneath us, a huge ash-grey mass. It looked very much like a bald rock sticking up, only there happened to be about two thousand feet of water under us. It was so big that I couldn't see beginning, end or edges of it. I yelled to my boatman to swing back but he didn't understand me and had to come aft to see what was the matter. By that time the kite was leaping and diving like a mad thing, the bait was a hundred feet in the air.

We never found the precise spot or saw the thing again.

To this day I haven't the faintest idea what it was, other than that it was very big and not a whale. A whale is of a greenish hue in the water.

Another time I saw some patches of what I thought was floating kelp. Under such patches, even far out in the channels, one often finds yellowtail and they are always hungry. We worked over toward the patches with the idea of dragging our bait past them. Imagine our astonishment when they bubbled and sank!

What were they? I don't know.

Now, there you have it; a huge, unknown creature, with enormous round eyes, and a reptilian head, lifting twenty feet out of the water; a great, ash-grey mass beneath us, almost within reach of the boathook; three patches of kelp that bubbled and sank before my very eyes; and lastly, which, if you please, you can put down to the vagaries of imagination, voices, bells and whistles at night.

Do you wonder that the sea plucks at one's heartstrings, calling one back, when things such as these lift up out of the depths?

MAGIC FINGERS

I CANNOT help being puzzled, and at increasingly frequent intervals, over what motive actuates the writing of these pages and why, after they are written, anyone should read them. The latter question, in so far as I am concerned, must, of course, remain unanswered. As to the other, however, certain possible reasons begin dimly to take shape and form.

It surely has become obvious that the sea and the fishing that goes with it have meant very much to me. It has brought interesting experiences and pictures whose vivid colors have remained unfaded over the years. Various lessons have been learned which have been pillars of strength upon which to lean in tight spots. And, over those same years, has grown the conviction that it is not the actual taking or killing of fish, either large or small, that makes the game what it is. Far from it! Instead, it is the background, all the little things one sees and does and hears, the sunrises and sunsets, the ever-changing face of the sea, the sheer loneliness of distant brooding islands, the strange, out-of-the-way corners into which the game takes one, the uncertainties, whatever elements there are of risk—or, in other words, the romance, the color, the adventure.

Strip fishing of these factors, and the thousand and one others, the enumeration of which space does not permit, and what have you? A deadly drab, uninteresting act wherein one goes out, throws into the water something on the end of a line in the hope that something alive will be fool enough to bite at it and thereby hook itself. Now, isn't that a fact? Isn't that all there is to fishing with the background taken away?

On the other hand, however, take that same act of going out and throwing a line into the water and, as a backdrop, paint in all the color, the romance, the adventure that Nature so abundantly provides, and you have something that sets your pulse a-stabbing—if there is a drop of red blood within you.

So, I think, it is that, gropingly, perhaps, I seek herein to pass on to others some of the joy of living which I have experienced out upon the sea in my years of fishing. To bring to others the rasp of salt air, the sting of wind, the touch of the magic fingers of the sun, which I have felt. Or, to put it another way, I seek to prove my case that "Out There" there is something to be had, and kept, something of vastly greater importance than a mere fish, or mess of fish.

It is a strange thing, this hold that the sport of fishing has upon men and women. Wherever one goes where fish are brought in one will find crowds gathered on the pier, at the boat landings, on the fish wharves. Very probably not half those interested spectators ever held a rod. But I'll venture to say that every mother's son of them wishes he had—and would, if he only had the chance. And I still maintain that it is something far more intangible than a dead fish, or boatload of dead fish, that holds the fascinated interest of those eager crowds.

It doesn't make any difference where one fishes—whether upon the sea, along the shores of a placid lake, or the banks of a brawling stream, if your eyes aren't dazzled by the beauty of Nature, if you don't find romance and adventure, then God help you!

Here, at one spot, is the rush and roar of white water tumbling over rocks to eddy out into a dark, mysterious pool within whose depths most anything may lurk. There is the first cast. The fly dimples the surface. Again it flicks. There is a boiling rush, a glimpse of something silver, the bending rod, the singing reel, and an iridescent creature leaping dangerously near the brush across the way. Or, at another spot, there is the burnished mirror that is a still lake at sunrise—the jumping fish—the spreading ripples—pines, tall and sombre, brooding at the very water's edge. Or, again, there is the wide blue sea stretching away to the world's end—the far horizon across which one's fancy leaps to countless other horizons beyond. There are the flashes of white water beneath screaming, milling birds—crescent fins, arrogantly weaving, lifting and falling over the marching seas—slender, sickle tails sliding down the purple swells into the shadow-mottled valleys between. Whatever the picture may be, wherever the canvas may be hung, it is all part and parcel of the same great game. And I give you my word, if you will only open your mind, that game will do things for you which are good. It will sweep away the cobwebs which befog the mind. It will correct and clarify the perspective of this vast painting called Life. And, in due time, years of peering across endless wastes of water, of attempting to penetrate the haze which veils the far horizons, teaches one to see a little further into the mists which shroud the horizons of life, to tear apart the veil, and see things as they *are*—not as one would like to think them. In the end it very frequently happens that one finds great things becoming small, and small things great.

Some of you who read may know precisely of what I speak. Others, lacking the opportunity, may not. So, for these others, or for anyone, for that matter, suppose we go out and see for ourselves. Live ourselves a day out upon the sea, hunting the big game which roam its depths. See with our own eyes the thousand and one little things which go to make up such a day. Determine for ourselves whether it is the fishing, or that which goes with the game, which makes it what it is.

Most of Avalon town is asleep. The fog has broken into lumps of brown grey clinging against the main ridges. The early sun seems to wash the dew-drenched scene with a golden light. White, red-roofed cottages climb the steep hillsides. The boardwalk, the graveled street is still damp. There is the sticky smell of salt in the air. The little flags hang limply. A few Mexicans, their voices rising and falling in the gentle cadences of their speech, perfunctorily sweep away the litter left from the night before.

Restaurants are filled with anglers. Windows are opaque from the warmth and steam. There is a cheerful clatter of dishes, shrilling of orders, that smell of smells—early morning coffee. The talk is of fish and fishing. Rumor runs riot. Tuna are here—they are there—they are somewhere else. One pessimist swears up and down they aren't anywhere at all! But he must be forgiven. Long days in rough waters, with never a sign of fish, have embittered his very soul, even to a point where life itself is futile—his friends, bores—himself, a wretched failure.

Then, too, the story circulates that bait is to be scarce this morning. That is the worst possible beginning of a fishing day. The weather-beaten person whose job it is to supply flying fish reported to someone that tides and currents were all wrong last night. "Th' fly' feesh, she no come in." It is also said that the day's allotment of bait will be but three fish per boat. That is worse than none at all! The Clemente Channel from San Diego Bank clear over to the island is teeming with hungry, hard-smashing tuna. A dozen baits would be none too many—but three—!

At the float are clustered half a dozen launches. They lie rail to rail, engines idling, as skippers gossip. Others come chugging into sight from behind the steamer wharf, their bow waves breaking the mirror-like surface of the bay and scattering the schools of tiny bait. Anglers stand about the wharf, talking, or lean over the railings peering down into the crystal clear waters where the rock bass, the spotted perch, and the flaming Garibaldis lurk. Others, their arms filled with packages, baskets and fishing tackle cautiously walk down the slippery gangplank to the float, ready to embark.

Our boatman is of a pessimistic turn of mind as all good boatmen should be. As a matter of good business it is far better to hold out little hope—then, if luck should come your way, he becomes a veritable miracle man, as much a magician as one who unexpectedly pulls a couple of rabbits, or a chicken or two, out of an innocent appearing hat.

" 'Mornin'," he grunts dourly as we climb aboard.

"No," this in response to our eager inquiry—"there ain't no bait to speak of. Told me I could only have three. Wa'n't that somethin'? Well, I fooled 'em. Snook a couple when they wa'n't lookin'! With what wuz left over yesterday that gives us 'bout a dozen. Oughto be 'nuff."

Then, and this always sets one's teeth on edge, "Where'd you say to go today?" This, too, is part of the "business." If you declare yourself for some particular location, and no fish are found, then it is your fault, not your boatman's. Just the old game of "passing the buck," and very, very useful when fish aren't plentiful. But with tuna everywhere, as they are today, it's silly. Any place in the Clemente Channel is as good as another and we say so, and ask what he has on his mind.

"Well," he says, taking off his cap and scratching his head, "it's just this away. Tuna wuz everywheres yesterday. But that ain't no sign they'll be everywheres today. Thought mebbe you might have some partic'lar place you wanted to go. Since you ain't, I got a hunch to go out to Far San Diego Bank. If there's tuna anywheres they'll be there—an' there won't be many boats 'round neither. What say?"

"All right, Cap, any place you say."

"O.K. then—but I'm afeared we ain't goin' to have 'nuff wind to hardly fly a kite—even th' big ones!" This last is just by way of dashing our optimism in case it had climbed too high.

Catalina's rugged coast line slips past us. There is queer Pebbly Beach, that keeps on building out to sea instead of receding. Its clumps of eucalyptus, the tent village, the ripped and scarred headland guarding its easterly end where the great rock and gravel quarries are. Fussy little engines, dragging strings of toy dump cars, cling precariously to the sheer hillside. There is a sudden mushroom of yellow, a dull "BOOOOOM" and avalanches of rock slide and rattle down to the sea as gulls rise and scold. Smoke from the ever-burning garbage dump lies in silvery slivers against the brown cliffs. The sea lumps heavily against bold Jewfish Point where the island swings to the southward. Through the haze astern unravels an endless panorama of bold headlands and broken mountain ranges. A few launches follow on behind us—three or four are outside a bit—and still others are ahead, the furthest being but indistinct specks in the fog.

Seal Rocks are passed. Giant seas roll majestically shoreward to break in a welter of green and white upon black, lime-washed rocks. A big bull sea lion roars out his challenge as we pass, his huge head weaving in angry petulance. "AWRNK! AWRNK! AWRNK!" The sound rolls and echoes against the cliffs, but certain sleek shapes, shading from wet, glossy black to dull brown, doze on in warm contentment, just beyond the clutching fingers of the angry surf. Perhaps his deep-throated roar is notice to the world that they are his, his own particular seraglio. To the south Church Rock lifts, and beyond that, fog veiled and lonely, is the San Clemente Channel.

Cap has been very busy sewing up baits. It's surprising what a complicated lot of sewing a flying fish requires if it is to stand up under the steady beating of being jerked and jumped along the surface. He straightens up and looks around. His gloomy forecast as to wind has proven groundless. There is a gentle breeze out of the south, just right for dragging a bait on our way out to Far San Diego Bank. He glances at the pennant on the forestay and hauls out a big red silk kite. Heading into the wind he climbs to the rail and tosses it up. For an instant or two it lags, darts back and forth, starts to dive, then, as a puff of air catches it, sails up and away.

"Might just as well drag a bug goin' out," he explains. "There ain't no tellin' what might pop up at it."

A "bug" is Catalina parlance for flying fish. And, incidentally, there you have one of the things that go to make the game what it is. "There ain't no tellin' what might pop up at it." True as gospel— and if it were not for that very uncertainty I wonder how many of us would stick with it a week!

The kite is up, the bait out, and the rod lashed to the chair—a tuna will pretty much hook himself on a kite bait that is working properly. So, there being nothing much at hand for the moment, we climb on top the cabin to look about, to be on the alert for a distant splash, or the glimpse of milling birds on the horizon.

Sitting atop the cabin, somehow or other a sense of the vastness of the sea seems to envelop one, or at least, so it does with me. The little boats are all scattered, far apart, each following his own particular hunch, or theory. Wherever one looks there is the mist-veiled horizon. And beyond that mist, across that line that seems to mark the boundaries of our world, what is there? Romance? Adventure? New scenes—new experiences? More than likely, but who knows for sure? And there again you have one of the things that make the game.

The fog is breaking up into grey-brown lumps—a very good sign. There will be wind enough, but not too much. It is a long run home from Far San Diego Bank and damnably uncomfortable if the afternoon slop is nasty.

The sea is changing color. The grey has deepened to a light blue —perhaps grey-blue, would be better. The long swells roll up from the southwest, their crests sun shot, the valleys between shadow mottled. Everywhere are cruising birds. High flying gulls—hovering, graceful terns, swooping shearwaters, at least I hope they are shearwaters. Anyhow that is what we call them out here—great broad winged fellows of brown and grey, with cruel beaks and yellow, staring eyes. How they contrive to swoop and bank, just missing the surface with their wing tips, is beyond me. If *we* knew that trick wouldn't *we* know how to fly! We come to one of those strange back alleys of the sea, that lane of dead water lying between the current drifts. It carries a greater collection of strange, outlandish stuff than you would believe; driftwood, boxes, half-submerged bottles, electric light bulbs, orange peel, an old hat, patches of floating kelp, some of which are so thick and matted as to make perfect roosts for sea gulls who teeter uncertainly on their precarious perch as their eyes comb the sea for the first sign of surfacing bait. Over yonder, just off there on the starboard bow, the surface darkens, flashed with darts of silver. Bait surfacing! The gulls take off from their perch upon the kelp. Other birds join them, racing to the kill.

Our flying fish skips along the surface, wriggling, jumping, skittering, creating a great commotion off there. It looks astoundingly life-like. Farnsworth certainly showed a flash of genius when he hit upon this method of fishing!

The island drops astern, losing the old familiar contours. In their place comes something new and unfamiliar—a roundish lump sticking up out of the sea, a sort of half moon with the flat side down. Just think of the countless other lumps sticking up out of the seas of this world. Wouldn't it be something to be able to go and have a look at them for one's self? That's my idea of high adventure.

Under the mass attack of sun and wind the legions of the fog have fled to the haven of the far horizons. But make no mistake about it. Let their age-old enemies once relax their vigilance, and back they'll be, creeping silently, relentlessly to veil again the visible world. But, in the meantime, the sky overhead is blue, and against it the red square of our kite forms a patch of vivid color. It nods and beckons and swoops as the breeze freshens, jerking the bait ahead in long, skittering lunges. Suddenly Cap stiffens and peers, shading his eyes. Presently, certain of what he thought he saw, he turns and grins, at the same time pointing.

"Tunny up ahead there!" he says. "An' travelin' deep."

It takes time—and a trained eye—to make them out. About a mile ahead there is the faintest difference in the appearance of the water, a shimmer—or shiver, it's hard to pick a word to describe it. It takes a long, long time for the eye to learn to discern tuna deep down and a mile or so away. But once the lesson is learned it is never forgotten, nor will tuna be mistaken for anything else. There are lots of things that look like them—wind riffles, for instance, tide rips, currents, cloud shadows. And all of us have chased these false signs.

But you will never mistake tuna for wind riffles, or tide rips, or currents, or cloud shadows. It was Enos Vera who said, "Win' she look like tunny. Tide she look like tunny. But tunny, she look like tunny!"

Well, anyhow, here we are and with a school of tuna just ahead. Our moments of restful reflection are gone. The next few minutes are filled with the bustle of activity. You must get the rod unlashed and get seated in the fishing chair. Cap is busy getting out another kite in case of a missed strike.

The school is close now. That queer, jiggly, upended motion of the water is as plain as print. Once in a while, from deep in it, there comes a flash of blue green as a fish rolls. They are traveling more or less the same way that we are. Cap speeds up a bit, heads them, then swings over to cross them. The kite has lagged as we eased down wind and the bait is dragging in the water with a bow of slack line behind it. Heaven help you if a stray fish should happen to smash at it now! There wouldn't be a Chinaman's chance of hooking him. But as soon as we are headed up again things are different. The kite leaps upward. The slack line straightens out in a hurry. The bait gives a tentative wriggle and skitters ahead toward that shaking water. A long sweep of the rod and it leaps into the air to splash back. Another sweep, another long skitter and jump and it smacks right down in the middle of it. We can see the brown backs—the blue-green flashes. It hangs for a second, then jumps ahead.

"SWISSSSSSH! CRAAAASH!"

The water parts. A live torpedo lunges out to crash down in a smother of white water. The rod jerks down. A green swirl eddies and spreads. The rod is almost snatched from your hands as the tip doubles down toward the water's edge.

The reel bursts into its throaty battle song. The kite line snaps.

[114]

The kite flutters down in graceful zig-zags. Your line is melting off the reel like magic. You are hooked on to a hundred pound tuna!

But that's enough of that. There are plenty of tuna fights in this book. This particular chapter of it is about fishing—not about fighting fish, or catching them. And so we will have to leave this fellow tearing downward for all he is worth and you hanging on to the rod and wondering when in Heaven's name he is going to stop. Perhaps, in the end, you get him. Perhaps he gets you. It doesn't matter. *Malaish!* Let's get on with our fishing.

Over yonder are a pair of little diving ducks. What infernal nuisances they are! How they seem to take positive delight in so lining up that, from a distance, they look exactly like the fins of a broadbill. How many, many times we have chased them, only to have them skitter away, their absurd little wings flapping madly. There is a saying that goes something like this.

"I saw a couple of broadbill today—but they had feathers on them!"

The wind is freshening and it is growing chilly up on top the cabin—too chilly for comfort. The big wicker chair down there in the cockpit looks inviting. From it the bait can be watched and you are ready to jump for the rod should anything "pop up."

It is nice to lean back and surrender one's self to the wiles of temptation—to let the magic fingers of sun and wind pluck at your drowsy eyelids. They are subtle and their magic is great. It works into the very core of your being and has you in its toils long before you are aware that it is working at all. Gently they pluck at *your* fingers, taking you by the hand and leading you off into a world of fourth dimension where there is neither struggle, selfishness, lust nor greed. It is a pleasant world, one of blue sky, of golden sunlight, of

[115]

whipping wind, of stinging salt, of white-topped hills sliding down into purple, mottled valleys. A world where all distances fade out into golden haze. Where the racing seas shout at you as they tear by, bidding you follow them home—home to where, at their journey's end, they crash joyously upon some lonely white beach against which they have thundered and beat since the world was made. Yes, it is a pleasant world into which those magic fingers lead you. But beware! Make very sure of what you are doing before you permit yourself to be led so far that there is no return. Remember, you, all of us, live in a practical world where facts are facts, and fancies not esteemed. And remember, too, that, whether you like it or not, in that practical world you are destined to live until *your* journey's end. If you do permit those magic fingers to lead you too far you will find that they will have left certain marks, certain scars, which will never heal. You will find yourself thinking along different lines from your fellows. Your sense of values will be altered. You will find yourself piercing the horizons which seem to be the boundaries of our practical world, and finding dimly, in the haze beyond—strange things.

Just to prove how powerful is the magic of those groping, plucking fingers, while we have been philosophizing they have led us into another sort of fishing—into new scenes and different waters. The raw channel wind is gone. The sea is smooth. The September sun is warm. Long ago the tuna have returned from whence they came. It is marlin time now and for those striped tigers of the sea we are fishing.

The towering cliffs of Catalina, their feet fringed with the white of surf, loom close at hand. The sea seems a bit overpopulated. Everywhere, close by and far away, are boats. There are big boats and little boats, and in-between boats—orthodox fishing boats—gilded things of putty, brass and paint commonly known as yachts—sea going schooners—hermaphrodite creations of no known design or pattern—whaleboats—yacht tenders—outboard skiffs. Each has its angler or anglers. Varnished rods flash in the sunlight. It's a busy, bustling scene, far different from the lonely waters into which the quest for tuna takes one.

A nearby boat whirls and stops, paying off broadside into the trough. Figures cluster in the stern. Off to one side there is a flurry of white water. Flick-flick-flick-flick-flick, a slender shape jumps and hits, jumps and hits. The boat swings and follows after. The rod flashes as the angler pumps and reels. Other boats turn and speed toward it. So do we. That's a marlin they're hooked on to, and there may be more of them there.

The boats gather closely around the lucky one—too close. The boatman shakes an angry fist at one overeager skipper and waves him peremptorily off. It's a cardinal sin to come too close to a boat when it is fighting a marlin or broadbill. One never knows where the fish may be. The fact that it surfaced in one spot is no sign that it is anywhere near there a minute or two afterward.

It must have been a stray fish they picked up, or else the school has moved on. Anyway, no one else gets a strike, and the boats fan out again. As for us, we head toward the Catalina Channel and its lee water. It is getting lumpy outside. The horizon line is broken, tumbled. Besides, it is nearly noon, and it's far more comfortable to eat lunch in still water. Cap is busy below and there is a comfortable smell of boiling coffee.

"SWISSSSSSSSH! SWISSSSSSSSH!"

A purple fin rips across the stern. A green swirl, a flash of purple, and the starboard teaser disappears.

"*Swordfish! Swordfish!*" you yell, reeling furiously.

"SWISSSSSSSH!"

Again there's that sound of ripping silk, that dark, racing fin. There is a swirl by your bait. Another! The rod jerks sharply and the line reels off.

"*Strike! Strike!*"

The reverse gear churns and grinds. Water boils up under the stern. The run slows and stops.

"*Hit him!*" Cap bellows.

You reel fast until you come up against something heavy, solid, then surge back, jerking sharply. Out there, astern and a little to one side, the water boils and out comes a slender rapier followed by a great wagging head and open jaws. For a minute or two he weaves and threshes, beating the air with his sword, then—

"RRRRRRRRRRRRRRRRRRRRRRRRRRRRRRR!"

He's off to the races. Straight for the island he goes, in and out of the water like a jumping-jack. You try to count the jumps. One! Two! Three! Four! Six! Eight! Ten! Fourteen! I think you missed one or two, but that's not surprising. Unless one has seen it for one's self it is unbelievable how fast a big marlin swordfish can go in and out of the water.

Finally the run slows. There is one more sullen lunge—he can only get about half way out this time—and then he changes strategy. Down he plunges into the deep blue caverns below.

And that is enough of that, too. You have been hooked on to a tuna and now you are on to a marlin. Didn't I tell you there was great magic in those plucking fingers? Anyway you are hooked on, fair and square, and are probably in for a tough time. Win or lose you are due for plenty of thrills and plenty of aches and pains as well.

But you will find out all about that somewhere else. Right now we are just fishing—peering, as it were, behind the curtain to learn whether it is the catching of fish, or other things, which makes the game.

We have worked well into the smooth warm waters of Catalina's lee. Our bellies are full. Deep contentment envelops us. The sun has started its daily slide down the slope of the sky. The golden haze of afternoon veils the island. Again those magic fingers pluck at your eyelids, grope for your hands. And again they lead you into other scenes and other waters.

It is another warm day. The sun, shining through the thin haze overhead, is hot. The sea is a rolling sheet of glass. We are on top of the cabin. Ahead, through the haze, buildings loom, and the fighting tops of battleships. San Pedro town splashes raggedly up the bare, brown hillsides. To westward stretch miles of chalky cliffs, a fringe of green vegetable gardens, and then the bare brown hills of the Palos Verdes lifting bleakly into the sky. A steamer swings around the Breakwater Light and heads west southwest for Honolulu.

"Say! What's that over there?" Cap exclaims. "Looks suspicious."

You strain your eyes toward where he points but see nothing. But yes—there is something there—something black. You just catch a glimpse of it before a big roller lumps up and shuts it off. Again it lifts. Yes—there it is—two black specks. Keeping your eyes fixed on the spot you grope for the glasses and try to focus them on it. But in the circle of the lenses there is nothing but rolling water. Slowly you sweep them back and forth. There it lifts again! Humph. Two birds sitting on kelp!

But wait a second. What's that beyond? A big sea rolls along and over its crest slip two crescent fins—a loafing broadbill!

"Keep him in sight," Cap orders and jumps down into the cockpit to make ready.

Nearer and nearer we approach those two cruising, crescent fins. He is just idling along. They weave arrogantly, leaving the dark line of a wake behind them.

"All right," Cap calls. "Come on down an' git ready for him. I see him all right. Looks like he might take a bait."

Now follows the exasperating circling—putting the bait in front of his nose—seeing him go down to look it over—and to surface again the picture of complete disdain. Perhaps he does take—although that is not likely. Even the magic of those fingers isn't quite up to the job of making a broadbill bite. If he does, though, you are in for hours and hours of gruelling work. Perhaps you will win— perhaps you will lose. But what difference does it make? One thing certain: you will have lived! You will have had your chance against the stoutest adversary man can meet on rod and line. If, as is most probable, he whips you, give him full credit for it. If, on the other hand, you whip him, more power to you. You will have done something. But, win or lose, no one can take away from you your days out upon the open sea—the colors of sea and sky and land, the cruising sea birds, the little white boats, the knowledge that, just over the horizon's edge, may lie adventure.

And now the magic fingers, having taken us into the world of the big three of the sea, take us still further to the lonely coast, the sunwashed beaches, the sweeping slopes of San Clemente Island. Abeam are gaunt skeletons of ruined frameworks—all that is left of the old, half-forgotten Mosquito Camp. A perfect flood of memories sweeps over us. Under our very eyes—and it may be that the magic fingers have something to do with it—those sagging, weather-beaten frameworks are again clothed in the white of canvas. Smoke lifts lazily from the cook house chimney. The sun has dropped behind the island as we head into the little bay. Half a dozen white fishing boats tug and strain at their anchors. Along the beach stand ghosts, the familiar faces of old friends long since gone down to the Happy Fishing Banks. They wave and shout their greeting. They are glad to see us—and we, them. What great tales there'll be of fish and fishermen when we are all gathered around the supper table that night—tales that will continue as, later, we sit and smoke upon the stone terrace and gaze thoughtfully out across the vast, mysterious sea. God grant that when our time comes, when our line has reached its end, we may leave behind us as fine a record as have they!

And still the magic fingers pull us onward. Clemente fades astern and lonely Santa Barbara looms through the fog, a saddle-back of rock lifting abruptly out of smashing surf. A more desolate, God-forsaken spot is hard to imagine, and yet there too, romance, hope, perhaps adventure, had their day. Atop that barren island stand rusty plows, cultivators and harrows. Who in God's name could have hoped to wrest a living from that sun burned, wind lashed heap of rock?

Then on we go toward Santa Cruz, pearl among islands. Santa Cruz with her tiny, land-locked coves, her beaches where impossible white stucco Italian houses peer through the sycamores at the end-less procession of purple seas marching down her channel. Santa Cruz of the "Painted Cave" wherein a fairly large boat might be taken with room and to spare—where, when the walls have finally shut down, there still can be heard from deep within the island the bark of sea lions—where the colors of walls and ceiling make mere words pitiful, inadequate things. But I have my own picture of Santa Cruz, and it isn't one of coves, or of incongruous ranch houses, or of painted caves. No, it's something else. It's a picture I once saw when I was coming in to the island in the late afternoon against a westering sun. The island was bathed in a mist of gold. Standing out against this mist was a ridge, topped with pine trees, marching down to the sea. That's my own particular picture of Santa Cruz.

We are getting pretty deep into the strange world of the magic fingers, too deep, perhaps, although there are many, many still further places for them to lead us. San Nicolas, the outpost island, brooding in its constant veil of fog. San Miguel where the great Cabrillo sleeps his eternal sleep. Cortez Bank where hungry surf sucks and sobs against the black reefs and the whistling buoy moans the whole night long.

But perhaps we have gone far enough. Perhaps we had best get back to our practical world before it is too late. After all, dusk is settling down. It's a long way back to Avalon town. The other little white fishing boats are hurrying home. We had best follow. We, they, all of us have had our day. We have seen and admired. We have been out into the "Great Lonesomeness." We have felt the kiss of wind and sun and salt. We have encountered certain magic fingers which have taken us into a strange and pleasant land. It is better that we get back to a world of practical facts before it is too late—before those magic fingers have too deeply marked us.

Now, I wonder. Is it the fishing that counts, the catching of fish, the fighting of them? Or, is it something else that makes the game? What do you think?

SERI INDIANS OFF TIBURON

THE VERMILION SEA

THERE is one thing about big game fishing. It does take one into interesting and lonely corners of this over-crowded old world of ours. Big fish don't grow on gooseberry bushes, nor will you find them in your garden fish pool. One must go out and hunt for them, but there is a lot of fun to be had out of that hunting, and a lot of punishment as well. There is the lash of wind, the glare of sun upon dancing waters, the sting of salt, the never-ending roll and pitch of a boat, and the punishing labor that comes with each and every fight. These things one must learn to take and like—and the funny part of it is that one does learn to like them perhaps better than all other things. Make of big game fishing a gentle, easy sport and you take everything out of it that makes it worth while. Take from it those days out upon the blue sea with wind and sun and salt for company—the sight of lonely wind-swept islands looming through the haze—the birds wheeling overhead—the ever-present uncertainty of what may be found just over the horizon's edge, and what is left? Nothing—absolutely nothing! But of all the fascination which goes with the game I think, perhaps, that the poking of one's nose into strange corners and strange waters carries with it the greatest thrill. And speaking of strange waters, here is one that is at our very elbows and yet they are few and far between who have visited it, or know anything about it.

How many of you have ever heard of the "Vermilion Sea"? I would venture the guess that not one in a hundred thousand. And yet the "Vermilion Sea" is a next door neighbor, but we know it as the Gulf of California, that deep gulf of lonely water lying between

[123]

the mainland of Mexico and the Peninsula of Baja California, and, I firmly believe, unequaled in all the world as a fishing ground.

Why the Spaniards gave it the name of "Vermilion Sea" I don't know, but no better name could be found. Its barren shores, the lonely islands that dot it, are desolate, forbidding, and the color of burned out, red brick. It is as though the fires from which our world was born had left those grim cliffs, those brooding islands, as everlasting monuments to the searing flames of creation. Venturing into that great gulf one almost immediately encounters a sense of oppression, of brooding loneliness, of the solitude that always mantles those parts of this world where men are few. From its discovery the old Spaniards wove strange, bizarre tales about it. Its depths were the home of unknown, fearsome monsters capable of crushing the stoutest ship as though it were an eggshell. The savages inhabiting its islands were half man, half demon, and skilled in the blackest of magic, and addicted to the most gruesome of orgies.

There is Tiburon, that great island lying some hundred miles north of the present port of Guaymas. God pity the hapless vessel that approached too near its shores! Those strange Indians of Tiburon, the Seris, were masters of evil magic. Once within the range of their spells the unhappy mariners were inexorably drawn to destruction upon its hungry reefs. Those unfortunates, living and dead, who were washed ashore fell victim to the cooking fires. But horrible as was that it was but the least of the terrible fate to which they were doomed. After their poor flesh had been consumed, and their bones scattered, their very souls were held in bondage, slaves to the black arts of Satan. When another ship approached, through the magic of the witch doctors these same wretched souls were again made to take on the semblance of living, breathing men, and to run up and down the beaches, holding out beseeching hands, and crying pitifully to be rescued. But woe betide those who listened to those cries! They, in their turn, fell victim to the savages, and joined their hapless fellows. Thus spake the old chronicles.

Of course, in the light of present day knowledge, such fantastic tales are ridiculous. But were they? There is never a legend but has some foundation in fact behind it. When one has ventured upon the sea long enough one sees and hears strange things. Dogmatism is weakened and one ceases to explain what fails of explanation.

Whatever seed of truth there may or may not have been in those ancient tales, the fact remains that the terrible Seris of Tiburon Island have most certainly fallen from their high estate—if they ever had one. I have been to Tiburon and have spent days with them. It taxes all one's powers of credence to even remotely believe that so miserable, ignorant and spiritless people were ever capable of any magic whatsoever. It is doubtful that, excepting the Australian Bushmen, and perhaps certain tribes in the interior of Africa, a more primitive people exist. Nor is it conceivable how any tribe or race living in such close proximity to modern civilization—Tiburon is probably not more than five hundred miles as the crow flies from Los Angeles—could possibly remain in such abysmal depths as have these Seris. They are down so low on the ladder of human progress that they do not even build habitations for themselves—not even brush jacales. Instead, they scoop a hole in the sand, lace a few bushes over it, and in that hole burrow men, women, children and dogs. They may be cannibals—I don't know. Certainly they look miserable and hungry enough to eat anything!

Wretched as they appear, however, debased as is their mode of living, there is something fascinating about them. It is as though they were a part of the prehistoric past come down the ages to rub shoulders with modern civilization.

There is but a pitiful handful of them remaining, probably not more than a hundred and fifty or so. They eke out their precarious livelihood by fishing and selling the fish to Mexican, Japanese and American fishermen. Soon they will have disappeared forever, sharing the fate of all their kind when civilization and progress brush against them.

They are an interesting people to observe. They are unlike any of the American Indians. The men are of moderate height, upstanding and with clean cut features. Young women and girls are not unattractive—or wouldn't be if given a good scrubbing. Most of them speak a little Spanish, or rather, Sonora Mexican. Apparently there is no mingling, no inter-marriage with Mexicans or with other Indian tribes. Even during the totuava season they live apart from the other fishermen.

Now here is something for the anthropologist to puzzle out—if he has not already done so. Tucked into their trouser bands the men all wear aprons, usually bandana handkerchiefs, and bearing an astonishing resemblance to that worn by Freemasons. How did that custom originate? What is its significance? I tried to find out but without success. Either they didn't understand me, or, and I had a strong sense of this, they didn't care to talk.

The chief of the tribe, and there was no doubt that he was chief, both from his bearing and the promptitude with which his merest word was obeyed, wears a most curious headdress. It is a framework of twigs, shaped precisely like the old fashioned tin dipper. It is worn upside down, with the handle sticking out in front. It is ornamented with bits of green, red and yellow cloth and string. Again, where could such a contraption have originated and what is its significance?

We men squatted in a little huddle and discussed where the big mule deer might be found. The women and girls kept their distance, eyeing us curiously and chattering gutturally among themselves, doubtless discussing us as women do strangers the world over. An old squaw sat in the sand hacking away at a totuava, cutting off its head. The knife was dull. The fish slipped and slithered until it was caked with sand. Presently she took the severed head, sand and all, and laid it upon some ashes. I put my hand on them and found they were only warm. After a little time she took it off the ashes, again sand and all, and handed it to the chief. Without ceremony he tore off the meat, and sand, with his strong white teeth, threw away what he didn't eat, and wiped his hands on the nearest dog.

When one is with them it gradually grows upon one's perceptions that the Seris do not beg. Gifts, such as fish hooks, tobacco, cigarettes, nails, fish lines, bread, flour, matches and so on, are gravely accepted with a courteous "Grácias, Señor." The closest approach to begging that I heard came from one old squaw. Bent almost double, leaning upon two sticks, she hobbled around the outskirts of our little group, mumbling through toothless gums, "No tengo tabaco! No tengo tabaco! No tengo tabaco!" The chief snarled something at her and she promptly fled away.

As for clothing they made use of anything and everything. The men wore blue jean shirts and pants. But with the women costume went the full range from the grandeur of typical, shapeless, dragging, Mexican skirts to astounding creations made from gunny sacks. One little girl's sole visible garment was an old cement sack. She was so sewn into it that the only way it could have been removed would have been to cut it off. Doubtless the theory was to let Nature take her course. In due time she would grow until she burst the seams. Until then, why worry? Men and women alike wore their hair long in two thick braids down their backs. In the case of the men these braids were usually interwoven with bits of colored string.

Like most primitive people the Seris exhibit complete stoicism in the face of hardship and deprivation. I experienced one vivid instance of this. We were anchored in a bay on the Sonora side, a little above the northerly tip of Tiburon. Most of the party was ashore hunting. About noon a stiff northerly blew up. Within an hour the sea outside was a smother of white. I could see the greater combers racing past the grim red headland that marked the point of the bay. Presently I caught a glimpse of the white rag of a sail rounding the point. In those waters the sight of a boat of any kind is an event and I wondered who in the world could be braving such a sea in so obviously a very small boat. Glasses didn't help much. There was too much sea and flying spume. Even the sea birds went whirling down to leeward. Presently the sail disappeared and I supposed that it had sought shelter under the point. I went back to my book and forgot about it until I heard voices alongside and scrape of paddles. There was a dugout canoe with seven Seris and I'll swear it hadn't six inches freeboard. They grabbed hold of the guard rail and one, a good looking young chap, climbed up and stuck his head over the side.

He smiled ingratiatingly and remarked quite casually,

"Tengo sed, señor!" ("I am thirsty"), adding in bastard Spanish they had been without water for three days and nights. That is a long time!

I got a two pound coffee tin and each of them drank it full and

[128]

half full. But there was no haste, no gulping of it down. They drank slowly and with dignity, as though they intended to enjoy every drop to the utmost. They drank in the order of their apparent age and those who were awaiting their turn did so without impatience, without even eyeing the drinker.

I asked the young fellow who still stood on the guard rail how it happened that they had been so long without water. He explained that it was five leagues from their camp to the springs on Tiburon which were their water supply and that it had been too rough to venture across the straits which separated them from the island. As the wind showed no signs of abating I found a five gallon tin, filled it with water, and gave it to them. They murmured their thanks for that and for the fish hooks, lines, nails, tobacco, matches, bread and flour I gave them. It was interesting to watch them distribute these gifts. Everything was divided into seven parts, even each loaf of bread, and each received his part.

After a few minutes of chatting about fishing and hunting they touched their hats and paddled off toward the shore with every sea breaking clear over them. They must be good seamen. Mexicans who know them tell me that they make voyages of a hundred miles and more in those dugouts. How they keep afloat I don't know!

I do not know if the Seris have been or are cannibals. Mexicans still tell hair-raising tales of their savagery. To me they appeared very peaceable. I had an uncle who spent much of his life in Sonora, Sinaloa and Baja California. During his wanderings he spent several months on Tiburon Island. This was more than forty years ago. Always he scoffed at the very idea that the Seris were cannibals, but added, with an eloquent shrug, "But, since they eat snakes, lizards, grasshoppers and ants, God knows what they do not eat!"

[129]

A strange people these Seris and extremely interesting. I could go on about them forever, were it not for the fact that this is a fishing book and people like them are but incidents which come with the game.

Game fish of the sea, and the pursuit of them, have been my hobby for a good many years. Concerning them I have read everything upon which I could lay my hands. I have eagerly questioned every angler I have met who, more fortunate than I, has fished in out-of-the-way waters. Summing up what I have learned by spoken word, and printed page, I will go on record to the effect that I don't believe that in all the world there is a fishing ground to equal for quantity, variety, or size of the fish, this Gulf of California, this "Vermilion Sea," which lies at our very back door.

Six hundred miles deep, three hundred wide at its mouth, it yawns directly in the paths of the great migratory game fish. Someone has called it "the greatest fish trap in the world" and that describes it perfectly. Into it, as into the mouth of a trap, pour the tuna, marlin, broadbill, sailfish, and the hordes of their smaller, but equally stout fighting migratory brethren, to join the still greater hordes of those who make the Gulf their home. Of these latter, just to mention a few, there are skipjack, bonito, dolphin, rooster fish, the big barracuda of the tropics, red snappers, amber jack, wahoo, yellowtail and their first cousins, the torel, a dozen different varieties of seabass including the hard fighting cabrilla and the great totuava, and cerro mackerel, golden spotted and beautiful, fast as greased lightning, and unequaled as a table fish. It is an actual fact that there are places in the Gulf of California where extra large bait must be used if one is to get through the multitude of smaller fish to the big ones below!

As for fight—well, it beggars description! Never anywhere have I found such ferocity. From the largest to the smallest they will fight you to the bitter end and only through main strength and awkwardness do you drag them alongside. Just why this should be I don't know, unless, perhaps, it is the over-crowded state of the waters and the furious struggle for existence which is forever carried on beneath the surface. Forget your light tackle when you go into the Gulf of California. I have broken twenty-four thread lines one after another on fish that didn't weigh twenty-five pounds. I have seen ten-pound cabrilla bass twist into a shapeless piece of metal No. 7 trolling spoons and straighten out heavy tuna hooks. I have had six-pound cerro mackerel rip off three or four hundred feet of twenty-four against the heavy drag of a big Coxe reel. I have seen twenty-five pound *cabrilla de la bahia* sit themselves down among the rocks from whence they had lashed upward to grab the bait and keep a strong man puffing and heaving on heavy tackle for two hours. In fact, I have done some puffing and heaving myself!

We were crossing from Keno Bay on the Sonora side to Bahia de la Cruz on Tiburon. At the south end of the big island are two smaller ones. The straits between are about two miles wide. Our boat was seventy-five feet and Diesel powered—far too large and clumsy to maneuver when hooked on to a fish. All that could be done was to check headway when a fish struck and lie to until he was pumped in. We were over two hours getting through those straits. It was strike-strike-strike as fast as a lure hit the water. One of the party was using my heavy tackle outfit—sixteen-ounce Shaver rod and 12–0 Coxe reel with eighteen hundred feet of twenty-four thread line.

Suddenly he had a smashing strike followed by a terrific run that just kept right on going. Of course, in time, the weight of the line slowed the fish down, but he kept on going just the same. As the line continued to pay off and the spool dwindled it became necessary to get overboard in a skiff and fight him from that. By the time the small boat was cleared away I don't believe there was three hundred feet left on the reel. We took out after him and in due time found ourselves more or less over the fish. Then followed about two hours of as hard a fight as I ever witnessed. The angler, while not particularly experienced, was a powerful man. The way he laid into that outfit—remember that it was mine!—made me shudder.

I couldn't for the life of me figure out what we were fast to. All the fish we had taken had been cerro mackerel and an occasional skipjack. It didn't seem possible that either of these was capable of so terrific a run or such a stubborn fight. He seemed to be circling something after the manner of a tuna, and Gilmore couldn't move him an inch. I began to wonder if perhaps we might have hooked up with a big yellowfin tuna, although the odds were all against it at that season of the year.

Everything seemed to go wrong. The gimbal rod socket snapped. I hurriedly nailed another to the thwart and that one promptly broke. Fortunately we had a leather belt socket aboard which I nailed down. It worked to some extent, although the rod persisted in jumping out and pinching Gilmore in sundry tender spots.

Dusk began to settle. The big boat, after standing by for a time, finally left us to proceed to the anchorage some two miles away before it got dark. Gilmore was growing tired. His hands, of course, had blistered and he was having difficulty closing them sufficiently to hold the rod steady. I think that it was only his certainty that he was fast to a very large fish that kept him up to the job at all. As for me, doubts had begun to creep in. When we had caught up with the fish I had taken bearings and it seemed to me that we were just circling around the fish, not the fish around us. In other words he seemed to be foul of something, although there was no kelp to be seen. Gilmore, on the other hand, was sure that he could feel movement and that the fish was making short runs. Suddenly the tip popped up.

"He's coming in!" Gilmore cried, grinding and pumping away for all he was worth.

I got the gaff ready, wondering just what I was going to do with a big fish in a skiff and two miles of rowing ahead of me. Faster and faster the line piled up. Peering down into the darkening water I caught a glimpse of a greyish-green mass. I rubbed my eyes and stared, scarce believing what I saw. That fish didn't look to be more than twenty pounds. I reached into the water, took him behind the gills and lifted him into the boat. He was a *cabrilla de la bahia* and weighed twenty-seven pounds!

Of course I don't think any fish of that weight could put up a two and a half hour fight on heavy tackle—but I don't know. There was no kelp, only rocks. How he could have become fouled in them without chafing the line I can't understand. Later on I learned more about cabrilla, although we never struck one that put up quite such a fight.

We spent two days in Bahia de la Cruz and never have I encountered such fishing; nothing very large, but such a variety of hard fighters running from ten to fifty pounds as I don't believe could be found anywhere else in the world. And hungry—I never saw the like of it! Why, you couldn't throw even an empty cigarette package overboard without something slashing at it.

As all anglers know, trolling spoons are designed solely for trolling. Without movement they are merely pieces of metal. One morning I was standing looking into the crystal clear waters beneath us and the great schools of fish milling around. Beside me a three-six outfit was leaning against the rail. On it was a Knowles Self-striker spoon dangling straight up and down and just under the surface. A big school of white seabass came along. There was an upward flash and one of them nailed that spoon. I had just had time to grab it before the whole outfit jerked overboard. I caught that fish and he weighed 37 pounds, but that isn't the point. The thing is that he *took that idle trolling spoon hanging in the water!* That is some indication of the savagery of those Gulf of California fish.

That same afternoon Gilmore and I went out in the tender. We were both using heavy tackle. The bottom of the bay is covered with clumps of submerged rocks—dark brown patches in the blue water. Every time our spoons crossed one of those patches we both had strikes. As soon as the fish hit they plunged back toward the rocks from whence they came. Of course, if they reached them, the chances were a hundred to one for a broken line. Obviously it was up to us to sit back and stop them. Sometimes we did—and sometimes we didn't! Time after time they broke those heavy twenty-fours on a straight pull. I never have experienced two hours of such fast action. In that time we brought alongside, between us, forty-two cabrilla, two or three cerro mackerel, one yellowtail and a couple of white seabass. At the end we were wringing wet with sweat, our hands were blistered, and, to be frank about it, we were both all in. And I don't think there was a fish in the lot that weighed more than thirty pounds. As a defense against a charge of needless slaughter, I might add that we were using barbless hooks and shook the fish off, unharmed, as soon as they were alongside. That afternoon taught me something. Pound for pound, cabrilla bass, ugly, mottled green fellows that they are, in fighting qualities are capable of holding their own with any fish that I have ever handled.

I have spoken of the desolate loneliness of the Gulf. Bahia de la Cruz was typical. There is the steep and narrow pebbly beach. Two valleys, filled with drab, grey-green mesquite open out upon it. Behind pile range upon range of barren, brick-red mountains as bare of vegetation as are the walls of a room. Toward twilight the island seemed to take on a quality of sinister brooding and it was not too difficult to give credence to the old tales of black magic, of cannibal feasts, of poor, bewitched spirits haunting the beaches. And when two wild dogs appeared out of nowhere and stood at the edge of the surf howling mournfully, one would have almost sworn those tales were true.

There is another picture of the Gulf that will always hang in my gallery of memories. We were lying on the Sonora side a little above Tiburon. With startling suddenness a Norther whipped down driving us out. The nearest shelter was an islet some ten miles to the southward. I don't know its proper name but we called it "Sombrero Island." From a distance it was exactly like one of those high peaked Mexican hats the cholos wear.

That island must have been the home port of every sea bird in the Gulf. Long before we reached it we joined the ranks of them winging their way toward it, in flocks, in columns, in lines, in ranks, singly, in pairs, in families and in nations. We came to anchor about three-thirty in the afternoon and still the birds swept past us. Until dark hordes of them poured by. Some, especially the pelicans, appeared to be about all in. Heaven knows for how many miles they had been fighting that furious gale! They would flap laboriously along, slide down to the water, rest a few minutes, then take off to flap a few yards further. I hope they all made it in the end. After dark we could still hear the beat of wings on every side. The din from the island shrilled above the howling of the wind and the crash of the heavy surf. As for stench—you never smelled anything like it in your life!

About eight o'clock the wind shifted, wiping out the scant shelter we had enjoyed. There was nothing to do but get out and run some fifty miles to the nearest protection we could be sure of, which happened to be Bahia de la Cruz. That run gave me one of the most beautiful scenes I have ever witnessed. The moon was full. Great seas, every one of them combing, raced down out of the north, turning the Gulf into a smother of white. Off to port, brooding, malignant, forbidding, Tiburon Island loomed, the angry seas throwing foam fifty feet into the air as they crashed against its rocky shoreline. Down that coast we rolled and wallowed and pitched and yawed. Shouting seas piled up behind, shouldering us up, twisting and throwing us, then sliding out from under, to drop us sickeningly into the dark, foam-streaked pits behind them—or, catching us under the stern, they threw us forward as we raced, almost bows under, down their steep slopes. That was a ride I shan't soon forget.

So far we have dealt only with the upper reaches of the Gulf. I think, perhaps, that that is because of the tremendous fascination which Tiburon Island, with its tales of witchcraft and cannibalism, has for me. As a matter of fact, however, it is down by the mouth of the Gulf that the real fishing is. There it is that one finds the great black marlin of up to a thousand pounds, perhaps more, the striped marlin of almost any weight within reason that you want to name, sailfish to two hundred pounds (Think of that, you Florida fisher-men!), tuna, yellowfin and Allison, to four and five hundred, rooster fish, torel and all the multitudes of other and smaller fry with which these waters abound.

Cape San Lucas, the tip end of Baja California, is a ridge of jagged, saw-toothed, lime-washed rocks reaching out into the sea. Under its shelter, such as it is, is the little bay and fishing village of the same name. Off the point, sometimes even within a hundred feet of the beach of San Lucas, and around the corner for a hundred miles up the Gulf are to be found the great game fish of the sea. Have the luck to be there when the fish are in and I'll promise you such sport as you never dreamed of, even in your wildest flights of fancy.

San Lucas comes pretty near to being the world's end. Its only communication with the outside world is by sea, by such boats as happen to go there for the fishing. It is a desolate, lonely place of a few whitewashed shacks, a tumbledown pier, and a low hill behind surmounted by a cross. Around that cross hangs a tale.

San Lucas lives for and by fishing. If it is good, the people eat. If it isn't, they don't. Years ago, to show their gratitude to the good God above and as an offering that He continue His bounty, the people erected a crude cross upon the summit of that rounded hill. For years thereafter fish abounded. Food was plentiful in the little homes. Fishing boats from Los Estados Unidos de Norte America to the north came down to base upon the little bay and to increase the profits of the people through trade. In time everyone had a few pesos wherewith to purchase luxuries at San José del Cabo and even to bring them from La Paz. Then misfortune in the form of a terrible chubasco—colloquial for hurricane—struck, and when the storm blew itself out the cross was down.

Now Mexicans are unlike Americans. We would have promptly rebuilt it, granting that we had ever thought to erect it in the first place. But not they! If it was the will of God that it should be blown down, then that was all there was to it. Who were they to question Him or seek to thwart His will? Instead they meekly bowed their heads and awaited whatever calamity that might ensue. They did not wait long.

With the ending of the storm and the destruction of the cross the fish disappeared. Day after day the men went out while the women prayed. Night after night they returned, empty handed and heavy hearted. The women wept a little as they prepared the frugal meal and prayed all the harder. But still the fish remained away and San Lucas was threatened with starvation.

Then, early one morning, into the bay sailed a big tuna clipper from San Pedro. On board was an executive of one of the large tuna packing companies of California. He knew these people and liked them. They on their side liked and respected him. Always he had been fair with them in his dealings. Now they hastened to him to pour into his sympathetic ears their trouble. He listened, smiled and bade them be of good cheer. All might come right in the end.

Forthwith he set the ship's carpenter to work building a new cross, twice as big and four times as durable as the first. When it was done he called the people together and presented it to them. A priest was brought from San José del Cabo. With him leading the procession the cross was dragged up the hill, set up, this time in a bed of concrete, and properly blessed. The very next day the fish returned in greater abundance than had ever been known before!

Now, there is no particular moral or point to this little story—other than that it is true—and that there are lots of decent people in

this world, particularly among fishermen. The man's name was Bismark Haussels. He is dead now, having taken the long traverse down
to the Happy Fishing Banks. I don't know much about such matters,
but we are told that it is St. Peter who keeps the Gate of Heaven
and before we can pass through we must first pass his scrutiny. Now,
if we read our Bibles right, St. Peter was a fisherman and must,
therefore, know fishing folk. I like to think that when Bismark
Haussels presented himself at that Golden Gate, St. Peter put out
his hand and said:

"Oh yes, Haussels, I know all about you. Never mind your cre-
dentials! Come on inside!"

The "Vermilion Sea"—a world in itself—a world of magicians,
of black arts, of cannibals, of strange monsters, of great game fish—
and, speaking of monsters, how many of you know the manta ray,
that great sea bat, sometimes twenty to thirty feet from wing-tip to
wing-tip? There is an ugly customer for you! Ugly in looks, ugly to
meet, as he weaves and rolls his way along, occasionally leaping clear
of the water to crash back with a noise like a cannon shot—one of
the truly dangerous creatures of the sea. Many is the story of attacks
by these mantas, of the crushing of small boats and the eating of the
unfortunate crews. If you want a thrill, harpoon one of them, and
take the ride he'll give you. But don't try it out of a skiff or small
launch!

The "Vermilion Sea"! As I look back there hasn't been so much
of fishing in this tale as of other things. But, after all is said and
done, it is really these other things which go to make up a good part
of the fascination of this fishing game. Poking one's way into strange
corners. What a world of romance and adventure is contained in
that simple phrase! I can tell you this. If you have never stood in

the bow of a boat as she noses her way into some strange cove, where you have never been before, you have missed a bit of living!

The "Vermilion Sea"! It won't be long now before its charm, its loneliness, its remoteness are gone. Soon the Gringo will swarm its waters. Guaymas is but a night and a day and part of another night from Los Angeles by rail and Pullman car. It boasts an ultramodern hotel and boats from which to fish. Sinister Tiburon is but a hundred miles to the northward. From it, across the Gulf and looming dimly, can be seen lonely Angel de la Guardia. San Lucas is four or five days from San Diego by boat, but only five or six hours by air. No doubt but that one of these days some enterprising and far seeing individual will there set up a fishing camp with adequate boats and accommodations. The day is not far off when the "Vermilion Sea" and the wild lands which border it will be known throughout the world, wherever fishermen and huntsmen gather. Then its charm will be gone forever. It will cease to be the "Vermilion Sea" and become just another bit of fishing water—just another part of the world where man can kill to his heart's content.

For the present, at least, may I offer a word of advice? Should the lure of adventure call you into those waters, provide yourself with ample reserve gear. You will find that you will need it and you will find, too, that nothing can be obtained there. Furthermore familiarize yourself thoroughly with the fish and game laws of Mexico. They are good laws, far better than most of those of our own states. Through their observance and proper enforcement Mexico will preserve that great outdoor heritage of hunting and fishing which we have so shamefully wasted. You will have no trouble in Mexico if you obey their laws, just as Mexicans have no trouble in our country if they obey our laws.

It is unwise to venture into the Gulf between July and October. That is the season of the chubasco. They come up very suddenly and blow with almost hurricane force. If your boat is big and able you can weather them all right, but you will be damnably uncomfortable.

Now—adiós to the "Vermilion Sea," its brick-red mountains and islands, its strange peoples and stranger legendary history. The lime-washed teeth of Cape San Lucas are abeam. We round them, take our departure and head northward into the teeth of the big Pacific surge.

Adiós y muy buenaventura!

"BROADBILL! BROADBILL!"

BROADBILL! *Right over there! See him?"*
There's the call for you to start the blood a-pumping. That brings you to your feet with a little tightening of the throat as you peer across the waters, shading your eyes from the glare, trying to get a glimpse of two haughtily weaving crescent fins. That brings the thrill of mingled hope and uncertainty. What will be happening in the next few minutes? Will he take it, or will he pass it up? Are you in for three, six, eight, ten, fifteen hours of punishment with the odds in favor of humiliating, bitter defeat in the end?

Broadbill swordfish! There's the fellow who can test you, find out what you are made of, force you to your ultimate limit, then make you find new limits to go to. What a fish for any angler! Big, tough, powerful, tireless, possessed of unbelievable stamina, sometimes bordering upon the dangerous—truly there isn't his equal in the Seven Seas. Granted that he doesn't seem to have the dogged, never-say-die qualities of the bluefin tuna. Granted that he doesn't tear all over the ocean, in and out of the water like a jack-in-the-box, as does the marlin. But, granting all that, take it from me he has plenty and I never yet had one of them come up and waggle a white flag under my nose.

A broadbill is not like other fish. Talk about your "rugged individualism!" He is the grandfather and patriarch of the clan. Neither in habits, nor actions, nor characteristics does he resemble any other fish. He isn't even like himself. No two fish behave alike. He does not school. He is the lone wolf of the sea. In my own experience I never remember seeing two of them nearer together than a quarter of a mile. You needn't crawl on your belly, and scrape it over rocks, for fear he will see you. On the contrary, he'll come to *you* and look you squarely in the eye. He doesn't give a damn for you and makes no bones about it. And for sheer cussedness he has every other fish I have ever encountered beaten a mile.

You don't even fish for him as you do for other fish. You stalk him. Day after day, in good weather and bad, you comb the ocean, never for an instant taking your eyes from its rolling, broken surface. The sun burns you. Wind and salt blister your face. Nights, when you close your eyes you still see those limitless wastes of moving waters.

A broadbill is very reluctant to take a bait. Experience, and I am confining myself to California waters in this, proves that about one out of every seventeen fish worked will strike. If one averages seeing two fish a day over a season's fishing, he has done very well. Probably about one out of ten or fifteen fish hooked is landed. Figure it out for yourself. Average seeing two fish a day—one out of seventeen worked (and you don't get a chance to work every fish you see by any means) will take a bait—one out of say a dozen hooked will be landed. Nice work if you can get it—but try and get it!

One of the most tantalizing things about them is their persistent refusal to take a bait. They will generally go down to it and they will generally take a look at it, but that is as far as it goes. There is not a one of us who has chased them who hasn't figured a dozen different ways to make them bite and not a single method has worked consistently. I think they are deep feeders and that when we see them they have already fed and are loafing on top, in the sun, content with the world and themselves.

In my opinion, of the Big Three—tuna, marlin and broadbill—

the latter is by far the hardest to hook, to handle, or to take. His
vitality is beyond belief. Let me give you an example. The late W. C.
Boschen, who took the first broadbill on rod and reel and who was
the father of the sport, if you want to call it sport, took an average
sized fish after about a three or four hour fight. When the fish was
gaffed they hauled him up upon the stern of the boat and lashed him
down. The run back to Avalon consumed about three and a half
hours. There was another half hour used in hoisting the fish from
the boat to the weighing standards. Just as they were about to weigh
him he came to life. He started threshing around, broke the rope by
which he was hung, smashed over one of the standards, which
weren't toys, ran everybody off the end of the wharf, knocked a piece
out of the rail, and plunked back into the water! And all that, mind
you, after he had been out of the water for over *four hours*.

I have said that broadbill are stalked, not fished for. That is correct. We don't fish until we see one. Then a barracuda, or a mackerel, is run out on about one hundred fifty feet of line. We then start
circling the fish, narrowing the circles until it appears that the slow
moving bait will pass fairly close in front of him. When it is about
there the boat is stopped and additional line paid out in order to
check the bait's headway. It slowly sinks down. The broadbill begins
to show signs of restlessness. His tail flicks. The dorsal fin twists and
turns. One can almost picture him studying that shining thing sinking in front of him. Suddenly the great tail lashes, there is a boiling
swirl and he has gone down to it. The next few minutes are tense.
There is nothing to see. The surface is smooth and unruffled. But
down there, fifteen, twenty, thirty feet, there is your bait and a great
fish.

I have watched them from a crow's nest and it is most interesting, looking down upon bait and fish and seeing all that goes on. Once down he swims slowly around the bait, twisting, turning, studying it from every angle, occasionally making tentative little rushes toward it. Sometimes he will go right over to it, pick it up crosswise in his mouth and swim away. Other times he will hit it a vicious rap with his sword and then pick it up. Most often, however, he ultimately turns contemptuously away from it and surfaces again.

I once hooked a broadbill—or thought I had. I hit him hard a number of times. He felt solidly hooked and began to sink. For three-quarters of an hour I worked on him very, very hard. Suddenly the line went limp, the tip popped up.

"He's gone!" I said.

"What happened?" the boatman asked.

"Hook pulled out, I guess. It didn't feel like a line breaking."

When I started to reel in it felt heavy, as though there were something still on. I began to wonder if the fish was still on and was coming straight for the boat as they sometimes do. But, when I got the swivel out of the water, there was the barracuda on the hook and intact. We hauled it aboard and examined it. The only damage was that it was pinched together in the middle. There is no doubt whatever but that this is what happened. He picked up the bait, swam away with it, and let me pull and tug as hard as I could. When he got tired of playing that game he merely opened his mouth and let the bait go!

Earlier I said something about an element of danger in broadbill fishing. There is, but don't let that stop you. A broadbill is big and powerful. Nature has equipped him with a wicked weapon of offense—that four-foot, two-edged sword. With it he does amazing things. I have seen him cut a barracuda in half, *in the water*, as cleanly as it could be done with a butcher's cleaver on a block. I have felt the wind from that sword whistle past my face when a fish I was gaffing reared up and slashed down. On Georges' Banks where broadbill are fished commercially and where dories are used to pick up the harpooned fish, every season has its toll of dead and injured. In the Paumotu Archipelago, in nearly every village on those coral atolls you will find men scarred, sometimes crippled for life, by broadbill swordfish which have attacked their canoes outside the reef. Down there the natives, backed up by white traders, claim that these fish reach the unbelievable lengths of eight and ten meters. I don't know whether they grow that large any place in the world or not, but I do know that I have seen broadbill in the Catalina Channel that I feel certain weighed as much as a thousand pounds, perhaps more. Now, any fish that big, and with as effective a weapon as that sword, *can* be dangerous. So far no tragedy has marred this fine sport. But one of these days it will happen. Mark my words.

There is another thing about broadbill. He is the one fish that I have had anything to do with which really seems to think. Time and again, after hours of fighting, I have had them swim deliberately toward the boat, bring up about thirty or forty feet off, and lie there in the swells watching us, seeming to study us. And never once when that happens has the fish failed to change his tactics. Time and again when I have been circling one I have had him keep turning away from me, keeping me on the outside of a circle, never giving me a chance to head him. Don't tell me they don't think and figure things out for themselves!

Back in 1916 I was keen after broadbill. It was a new game then. But one or two fish had been taken. We knew practically nothing about them—we don't know much more now. Tackle was inadequate. Our lines broke at about fifty-five pounds. The present day flexible cable leader was unknown. Instead we used heavy piano wire. It was strong enough, but inclined to kink and break.

We started across the channel early one morning. Broadbill seem to like to follow the lane closest to the mainland, about five or six miles offshore. It was the middle of July and we were having a spell of hot, windless weather, ideal for this kind of fishing.

About seven miles off Point Fermin we sighted the fins of what appeared, even at a distance, to be a very large fish. They were so high out of the water and so large that at first we thought we were mistaken, that it was two men in a rowboat. But the glasses soon dispelled that doubt.

"What a hell of a fish!" Cap exclaimed. "Want to try him?"

I attempted to act insulted, although, to tell the truth, the closer we came to him the less sure I was about it. The distance between fin and tail seemed to be all of twelve feet, and the fins, themselves, were at least a yard high. He paid not the slightest attention to us, apparently concerned only with his own business.

We started circling, a barracuda out for bait. Still he paid no attention, even when the bait dragged past and near him.

"We ought to lay it right smack in front of him," Cap announced. "As soon as I kick out the clutch you start peeling line off."

The water was so still and clear that I could plainly see the bait shining about a hundred and fifty feet astern. Unless he turned away it would pass within ten or fifteen feet of him. Nearer and nearer it came, flashing and twisting. Cap threw the clutch and went into reverse to check headway. I let the drag go free, just thumbing the line enough to keep it from backlashing. I could still see the bait sinking slowly and very close to the fish.

The fish stopped. The high dorsal twisted. The big tail flicked. There was a little swirl and he sank.

Cap jumped back to the controls.

"He's after it!" he shouted. "Holler if you feel anything!"

For all of five minutes nothing happened. The line lay in the water slack, wavery, sinking slowly as it became soaked. Bait and fish were out of sight.

Suddenly I felt a gentle tug. It was more as though the line had brushed against a jellyfish, or a piece of floating kelp, than a strike of any fish. But I yelled just the same.

"He's got it, I think!"

"Let him have it—all he wants!" Cap ordered.

I started pulling line off the reel. The weight of it ran it through the guides but it still lay looped and slack in the water.

Then suddenly I was conscious of something. Those loops and whorls were straightening out—and moving off to one side.

"He's got it! He's got it!" Cap shouted, dancing up and down. "Let him have it! Feed it to him! Don't hit him 'till I tell you!" He speeded up the engine a trifle and took hold of the clutch lever.

The line paid out faster. Something had hold of it and was off with it—off to starboard in a sort of big bow. Faster and faster it went. Cap jumped aft beside me narrowly watching the line and the growing speed with which it was being taken out.

"Better hit him!" he suggested. "Set up the drag and I'll kick ahead. When you feel him solid, sock it to him!"

The water boiled out from under the stern. The bag in the line straightened. I felt a tremendously heavy weight. The tip jerked down.

Grabbing the rod with both hands, thumbing the line just above the reel, I surged back once—twice—three times. I might as well have jerked against a rock. Then something happened, something that caused both of us to yell inarticulately.

About three hundred feet off to starboard the water parted and out lunged a great wagging head, jaws agape, and broadsword furiously lashing; beating air, water, himself! Somehow or other he had knocked the barracuda off the hook and it had slid up the leader to the middle swivel. There it stuck and was slapping and beating against his side just behind the gills. It appeared to infuriate him. He leaped and lunged and rolled, twisting and turning, slashing backward at it with his sword. Five times he lunged clear. There was none of the twisting grace of a marlin's leap. Just a sullen lunge and an awkward smash back—but words are utterly inadequate to describe the irresistible power, the insensate fury—or was it insensate?—of those smashing jumps. And there was something else, too. Something that left us both goggle-eyed and speechless. The monstrous size of him! When he came out we saw everything he had—his length, his breadth across the back, the depth of him. Never in our lives had either of us dreamed that there was such a fish in the sea. Then and there a feeling of hopelessness came over me—of the utter futility of anything within my feeble power to do against so huge a creature.

For about five minutes he fought the leader, the slapping barracuda, then took off, still on the surface, rushing around us in a great circle. There was nothing we could do but spin around on our tail and try to keep the line from running too far forward.

For perhaps fifteen minutes he kept this up, then lunged out once more and started to sink. Right at that point I learned something new about fishing. I braced myself for a furious rush downward, such as a tuna or marlin would make. But it didn't come! Instead, he seemed to just settle down. The reel barely turned over. For the moment I thought this was going to be simple. All I had to do was to tighten up the drag and stop him. I might as well have tried to stop a sinking whale! The tip doubled down to the water's edge. The whole outfit was nearly dragged from my grasp. I think it would have been if I hadn't released the drag in a hurry.

Down, down, down he sank, slowly, deliberately, almost arrogantly. Nothing I could do made the slightest impression on that slow sinking—even checked it for a fraction of a second.

"RRRRRRRRR! RRRRRRRRRRRR! RRRRRRRR!"

I was compelled to ease the drag still more, utterly incapable of standing that relentless down drag. I looked at the reel. About five hundred feet were out. We had headed around and were following him. The line entered the water just a little forward of the counter. I had had to swing my chair around until I was facing a little off the starboard bow. I looked at my watch. It was ten-thirty. We had hooked him just a minute or two before nine-thirty.

Cap came aft and studied the size of the remaining spool of line.

"See if you can't check him," he suggested.

I tightened up as much as I dared with that much line out. The tip doubled down again. Then, slowly, almost imperceptibly, the sinking stopped. The line began to move away from us a little. Cap speeded up, following.

I worked hard and found that I could get a little back. He seemed to be yielding to the pressure—sullenly, unhurriedly—but yielding just the same. I redoubled my effort and regained perhaps fifty or a hundred feet when the tip jerked down again.

"RRRRRRRRR! RRRRRRRRRRRR! RRRRRRRR!"

[151]

I strained and heaved. Not an inch could I get. He seemed to have leveled off and was cruising slowly out to sea and toward the island. By running at about a mile and a half an hour we found that we could hold our own. By speeding up a little more I could gain some line but we soon found that such tactics merely resulted in taking us right over him—a very bad place from which to fight a fish. Of course I did gain a few yards once in a while, but usually lost them again. To be honest about it I was utterly helpless. Whatever I did apparently made little difference to him. He kept on an unswerving, leisurely course directly toward Long Point on Catalina Island. It was as though there were a path down there and he was following it.

We had been on over two hours and were getting nowhere. Cap came aft and scratched his head, inviting suggestions. Obviously he was as nonplussed as I was.

"What d'you think we could do?" he asked. "It's a cinch we ain't gettin' nowheres this way!"

I had nothing to suggest. As a matter of fact I had long ago made up my mind that there was nothing either of us *could* do; that we would remain hooked on to that fish until something carried away, and then go home. Furthermore, I was growing very tired. I had worked hard, probably much harder than ever before on a fish. Every muscle in my body seemed to ache. My hands were already blistered. And then, to top it all, despite my every effort, the use of every trick I knew, I hadn't even fazed him. I was a pretty discouraged angler about that time!

I eased up—I simply had to—and looked around. Off to eastward there was a boat. From that distance we couldn't tell if it was an Avalon boat or not. The sea was still smooth but for a lazy north-

[152]

west roll. But it didn't promise to remain that way. Up to westward there was a smoky look. The Palos Verdes hills had dropped astern and were indistinct in the haze. Catalina's whereabout could only be guessed at. There were a few schools of bait about and some birds.

"RRRRRRRRRRRRRR! RRRRRRRRRRRRRR!"

He speeded up. Line raced off the reel. Where it entered the water it was moving rapidly away from us. He was surfacing.

"Cripes! What d'you know about that!" Cap yelled.

Out where one of the schools of bait was milling the water boiled and a black sword threshed back and forth throwing the mangled sardines every which way.

"Good God A'mighty!" Cap's voice was cracked and his eyes bulged. "He's feedin'!"

That is the absolute gospel truth! After all my pumping, reeling, straining, tugging, heaving at him for nearly two hours and a half, he came up and went to work on a school of sardines! Then and there I knew I was whipped! I honestly believe that that fish didn't know he was hooked. Doubtless the leader, the constant pressure, may have annoyed him a trifle, but that was all. Has anyone ever heard of a fish which has been hooked and fought for two hours and a half coming up and feeding? Well, I never have, before nor since.

For some reason or other Cap, after his first astonishment, seemed to find something funny about it.

"Heh-heh-heh!" he chuckled. There was something about that chuckle of his that used to drive me mad, it was so superior. "Now what d'you think 'bout these here fish? Can you beat that?"

I don't know what it was, unless it was that laugh, but I got mad all over and really gave that fish hell for ten minutes or so. I didn't accomplish much other than to drive him out of that school of bait and down again. Or, perhaps, he had had all he wanted. Anyhow he sounded once more and picked up his course for Long Point where he had left it off, we following along at about a mile and a half an hour.

Pretty soon Cap came back to me and stood watching the laboring tip and the taut line for a few minutes, thoughtfully scratching the two day stubble on his chin.

"Say," he remarked presently, "did you get a good look at that bird?"

I nodded.

"Got any idea how big he is?"

"What have you got on your mind?" I asked. Cap isn't very conversational as a rule when a fight is on.

"Well, I dunno as I got anything," he replied, spitting over the side. "But I seen a lot o' fish in my day an' this bird's got anything I ever seen licked. If he don't go a thousand pound I'm a Dutchman!"

For all I know he might go a thousand, or two, or three. It didn't seem to make much difference. Whether he weighed a thousand pounds or a hundred I couldn't do anything with him. Of one thing I was morally certain. I wasn't ever going to land him!

I still get cold chills when I think of those next two hours. Aided by Cap's superlative handling of the boat I fought that fish as I had never fought before. There were times when I didn't think I could stand it another minute. The blisters had broken. Salt water had run down the rod and into them. The constant twisting of the handgrip had turned them raw and bleeding. Sweat poured into my eyes, blinding me. Salt water dripped off the line, into my lap, and down upon the floor. My feet slipped and slithered. The chair spun and jerked. I grew dizzy. Horizons seemed to spin crazily. It was as though I were all alone, in some strange world, a world of pain and never ending down drag. From somewhere far away I could dimly hear certain sounds. By intense concentration they resolved into the chugging of the engine and words of encouragement from Cap.

Then, imperceptibly, I sensed a change. The steady forward pull became more intermittent, broken by short, jabbing rushes. It seemed, too, as though deep down there he was rolling, threshing. Cap was beside me. His voice in my ear.

"You been hooked on six hours now," he rasped—I think the strain had begun to tell on him, too. "What you goin' to do? Stay out here all night?"

The veiled sarcasm of his words filled me with rage. But I simply hadn't the energy to lash back. How should I know how long we would be out? It wasn't my fault if we were tied on to a huge, unconquerable brute. But my anger did me good, just the same. The horizons stopped their spinning and I seemed to gather new strength.

"Anyways," he went on, "I just wanted to tell you the wind's comin' up. That ain't goin' to make things no easier."

I suddenly realized that such was the case. The glassy sea had gone. Instead, we were surrounded by white caps. The wind whipped and whistled. That meant that soon there would be nasty breaking seas—hard water out of which to fight a fish, especially a big one. I dug in harder than ever.

During the next hour I gained perhaps fifty or a hundred feet. The short rushes, the rolling, seemed to have stopped. The fish seemed to be just a sullen, dead weight. Cap was back beside me again. He took off his cap and scratched his head.

"I got a hunch that bird has died on you!" he announced—although somewhat doubtfully. "Does he feel like he was movin', or anything?"

The answer was no, although of course it was hard to say with any degree of certainty. I would gain a little line and then lose it again. But it seemed more as if the seas, rather than the fish, were responsible for the latter. It was getting pretty rough. As is usually the case when fighting a fish we were in the trough and had to stay there. We were thrown about pretty badly. Furthermore the line went straight down over the stern. We were standing still, the engine idling. Cap threw in the clutch and we tried to move away a little. The only result was that we lost thirty or forty feet. As soon as he stopped and I went back to pumping we were right on top of him again. Cap came aft again looking thoughtful.

"How're you feelin'?" he asked.

"So-so. Why?"

"Well, I'll tell you. That fish *is* dead down there. It's goin' to be a hell of a job to pump him up. 'Specially with this kind o' sea runnin'—and it's goin' to get worse. He's awful damn big an' heavy. We can't afford to make no mistakes. If you take it slow, just 'bout half a turn or so of th' reel at a time, we might get him planin' up. How much line's out? Eight hundred feet or so?"

"I think somewhere about that much," I answered, adding, "but I don't know if I'm going to be able to pump this fish up any eight hundred feet!"

"Well, all you can do's the best you can. Just be satisfied with a few inches at a crack 'till you get him planin'. Watch these seas all th' time. I'll try to help you s'much as I can, but it won't be much!"

Cap knew what he was talking about. The fish *was* dead, and deep down, and it was going to be one ungodly job to pump him up. Perhaps after four or five hundred feet, provided the tackle and I stood up that long under the strain, he might start planing upward. But that first four or five hundred feet were going to be just plain, unadulterated hell.

I try to forget those next three hours. Inches at a time I would get a few feet of wet line back on the reel, only to have a combing sea rip it away from me again. I tried loosening the drag while we ran off for a better angle. But as soon as I tightened up and went to work again we soon found ourselves on top of him once more. We tried to tow him into the lee of the island—about three miles away —where the water was smoother. But it didn't work. The fish was too heavy and I was too tired to hold him. Besides, the leathers of the drag began to slip. They would catch and hold for an instant or two, then give way with a jerk that was punishing.

Cap brought me a dipper of water. It was lukewarm, but tasted like nectar. I gulped some down, but slopped most of it over my chest. What was left he poured on my head. Then he lit a cigarette and gave it to me. The combination seemed to help. A little of the numbness of extreme fatigue seemed to disappear. I found that by watching the seas, letting them do the lifting, then reeling as we slid off them, I could get line with less effort. It began to pile back on the reel in those old, familiar, and always welcome, wet, irregular ridges. By thumbing just above the reel it was possible to overcome some of the slipping of the drag.

I looked at my watch. It was six o'clock. We had been hooked on for eight and a half hours. The sun had sunk behind the island and dusk was beginning to settle. The island itself was like a brooding, purple monster. Long shadows began to creep out from it across the sea. I was growing desperately tired again. That second—or fourth—or fifth—wind that had helped me for a little time seemed to have left me for good and all. The rod twisted and slipped in my hands. The sea was sloppier than ever. It is always that way for a while after the wind dies. But in spite of everything—in spite of myself—I was gaining line. It was piling back fast—feet, even yards, at a time. The fish was at last planing upward.

Despondency, fatigue, aches and pains, all left me. It looked as though we were going to win. Cap was whistling and busy getting out the big gaff—a sure sign that he thought the end was near. He was superstitious about that. Never would he get a gaff ready until he was practically certain that a fight was won.

The fish was coming in fast. The two hundred foot marker came out and on to the reel. Instead of pumping desperately for every inch it was now more a matter of picking up slack. The line as it entered the water was steadily moving away. In a minute or two the fish would roll up on the surface.

My blistered hands, the cramped muscles of my forearms, made me awkward. There were times when I couldn't seem to keep a tight line. On one of these occasions I felt a series of three or four queer little jerks.

"Something's happening!" I shouted.

"What's th' matter?" Cap demanded, jumping back beside me.

Before I could answer there was another moment of slack line. I tried to pick it up. Just then a cross sea caught us and hurled us ten feet. There was a sickening snap and the line went slack for good.

I couldn't move—just sat there holding the rod and staring stupidly at the limp line hanging from the tip down into the water. Cap snapped his fingers.

"What th' hell!" he asked tonelessly. "Is he gone?"

I nodded.

"I'll be go to hell! What happened?"

I didn't know then, but I did in a minute or two. When I reeled in the empty line about three-quarters of the leader was left, and half of that was coiled into as perfect a spiral spring as you ever saw. During those hours of threshing and rolling, of beating with his sword, the fish had wrapped the piano wire leader around and around his sword. For hours I had pulled against those wrappings, drawing them tighter and tighter and tighter. As long as a tight line was kept everything had been all right. But, when he began to plane upward, gathering speed as he came, and I was unable to keep up with him, one or more of the loops had slipped off. The next heave tightened the first one into a kink. When that sea tossed us, the kink broke. That is all there was to it.

Without a word Cap spun the wheel and we headed home for the lights of Avalon. I threw myself down on the seat, physically and mentally exhausted. I had mechanically glanced at my watch when the fish broke off. It was seven o'clock. We had been on for nine and a half hours, or thereabouts.

I know a lot more about swordfish now than I did then. I have hooked on to my share, have caught my share. I have seen some big fish. But I'll say this in all truthfulness. Never before nor since have I seen as large a broadbill swordfish as that one. After a time, when the bitterness of having missed by so narrow a margin had worn off, I began to take stock and as I did so, felt somewhat better.

After all, it had been a very big fish. I had fought him hard and throughout the nine and a half hours. There had been no resting, no laying the rod down on the cockpit combing, no harness. In the end he had been killed. Whether or not that was the result of my efforts doesn't matter. If I hadn't hung on and fought for all those hours he wouldn't have been killed. With a cable leader I would have had him. Another ten minutes and he would have been alongside and a rope around his tail. I hope that, if I seem to hold myself in some small degree of esteem, the fact that it was really a very big fish may be credited in my favor. Ordinarily, I don't like to kill anything that can't be used. In this case, however, I must confess that I am not shedding too many tears over that phase of it. The remembrance of the sight of that fish feeding on sardines, after I had been fighting him as hard as I knew how for two hours and a half, still rankles. I don't mind being knocked down by a better man than I am, but I hate like the devil to be kicked afterward. In any event, he and his brethren were fully revenged upon me. It was in 1916 that I lost that fish. It was in 1924 that I landed my first one. Eight years to get one fish! And during those eight years there was many and many a time that I went home through the gathering dusk with naught but aching muscles, a bent and twisted rod, and a broken line to show for hours upon hours of hard, painful physical effort. But that's broadbill fishing, and that's why we love it, stay with it, and take the knocks. It's a grand game, but don't start it unless you are willing to go the limit in giving everything you have.

Alma Overholt, Santa Catalina Island

ISTHMUS BAY, SANTA CATALINA ISLAND

MORE ABOUT BROADBILL

FOR two seasons I fished with a man named Harry Adams out of his boat *Angler*. Harry was a great rodman, a very interesting character, and pure gold clear through. A typical "Maine man," much of the bleakness, the granite of his native state, was bred into the bone of him. His life had been one of hard work. Lumberman in Michigan, rancher in Arizona, cattleman in New Mexico, always he had been a driver. When his stake had been made, when the years came when he could play, a driver he still remained. Big game fishing, particularly for broadbill, was his hobby, and he drove at it just as hard as he had ever driven during his years of work.

It was no soft, perfumed fishing that we had. Never in my life did I do such hard physical work—or have so much fun in the doing of it. We lived aboard the boat, sometimes staying out at the islands a week, two weeks, even three, without coming into port or setting foot ashore. Four o'clock in the morning saw us up. By six we would be on our way. Seldom were we back in Avalon before five. A run of thirty or forty miles to where we had heard that fish could be found was nothing. Coming home through the rough water of afternoon, however, was something else again.

To my mind the *Angler* was an ideal fishing boat. She was thirty-seven feet long, had nine feet beam, and a draft of five and one-half feet. Many was the time I was glad of that deep fin beneath us. She was squat in the stern, but with a high bow and beautiful lines forward. It was bad water when we took them green over the bows. She was powered with a two cylinder, sixteen horse-power, heavy duty Frisco-Standard gasoline engine. Of course she was slow. You couldn't squeeze more than seven knots out of her to save your life. But that was all right. Long experience has taught me that with a fast boat you run over and pass up more fish than you see. Furthermore that engine always ran, and that's something when you are away out on Cortez, or Tanner, or Osborne Banks, anywhere from eighty to a hundred miles offshore, or on that desolately lonely ninety mile traverse between Santa Cruz and Catalina Islands. She bunkered three hundred gallons of gasoline, twenty-five of oil, and sixty of water, enough for three weeks if we wanted to stay out that long. As far as food was concerned there was space enough for a year's stores.

From the cockpit a companionway led down into a combination engine room and galley. Forward of that, on the starboard side was a lavatory and on the port a clothes locker, with an alleyway between. Then came the two-bunk cabin which led into the lazarette, general stowage and chain locker.

Avalon fishing boats, and I doubt that there are any better in the world, are all equipped with what are known as "jitneys." These are contraptions very much like the cab on a truck, only reversed. These extend forward a few feet over the cabin trunk, with front and sides glassed in. A sort of canopy, or rigid top extends aft to shelter the cockpit partially, but leaving the fishing chairs out in the open. They stand high enough to allow a splendid point of vantage for looking for fish. The top of the cabin trunk underneath the "jitney" is locally called the "bridge deck."

Harry kept tinkering with the *Angler* until he had about as perfectly appointed a fishing machine as I ever saw. The two after stanchions supporting the "jitney" were removable, leaving the roomy cockpit unobstructed when hooked on to a big fish. In the cockpit stern were three sockets for fishing chairs, two on either side and one in the middle. It was only a matter of an instant to pull out one chair, set the other in the center socket, and there you were. Upon the stern deck which was also roomy and with a removable pipe-railing, there was another chair socket. That was a perfect place from which to fight a fish unless the sea was very rough. On the bridge deck were rod, gaff and kite racks, kite line reel, and a locker for gear such as hooks, leaders, swivels, wire cutters, pliers, screw-drivers and the like. Below decks were reel and line lockers and racks for spare rods. Everything had a place and that place was where it could be reached the quickest, a most important factor in big game fishing where split seconds count. On the mast, about fifteen or twenty feet above the water, was a crow's nest. It was astonishing what one could see from up there and how the shadows flattened out. But it was a brute of a place in a lumpy sea.

So much for the *Angler*. My excuse for such lengthy description is that description of the boat will be of help in visualizing the word pictures drawn. Furthermore, to the dyed-in-the-wool angler it may be of interest.

Harry's dream of Heaven was to be hooked on to a hard fighting broadbill. I get mad all over again when I think of the schools of magnificent tuna we passed up cold on the slim chance that we might run across a swordfish. But at that we caught our share of tuna. In fact, during those two seasons we caught perhaps more than our share of all three—tuna, marlin and broadbill. And one thing we did become—a smooth-working, well-oiled machine. Often during a long fight there wouldn't be a word said for as much as an hour. Each knew what the other wanted and did it.

As soon as a fish was hooked, if Harry happened to be on the rod, first the big gaffs were brought out, the lines coiled and the ends made fast. The two after stanchions were taken out and stowed away on the bridge deck. A pitcher of water and glass were brought up and put into their rack—Harry consumed prodigious quantities of water when fighting a fish. Folding chairs, all cockpit impedimenta were stowed on the bridge deck, out of the way. The engine was switched over from magneto to battery to prevent it from killing at some critical moment. I would bring up my old frontier model, single action, Colt 45, in case of sharks. By then we would be ready for almost any eventuality.

Broadbill appear in Southern California waters in June and work slowly westward up the coast. Sometimes they stay for weeks upon some particularly favored bank. Ultimately they all seem to reach the lee waters formed by Anacapa, Santa Cruz and Santa Rosa Islands. There they gather in a sort of convention, sometimes lasting for as much as two months. September and October are the best months and, considering the scarcity of the fish throughout the season and further down the coast, their numbers are unbelievable. One wonders where they all came from. In one day I have seen as many as forty-five fish.

In September, 1923, Harry and I were at Smugglers' Cove at the east end of Santa Cruz. That year there was a veritable floating "town" up there—such a one as Kipling described in "Captains Courageous." Albacore were running out on Santa Rosa Flats, that forty mile bank that extends from Santa Rosa Island clear out to San Nicolas. The fish were none too plentiful and prices were high—as much as $400.00 a ton. As a consequence almost everything that would float was up there. There were big purse-seiners, staunch

"Montereys," powerful, clean-lined Japanese live bait boats, tiny one man jig boats, and strange, misshapen arks that made one wonder how in the world they ever weathered the passage up.

With the fleet came the cannery barges, each bearing its big sign of "CASH FOR FISH," and being sort of floating general stores. Of course their fundamental business was that of buying fish for their own particular cannery. But from them could be had provisions, tobacco, candy, hooks, lines, jigs, some notions, daily papers and mail. Every night at about eight o'clock the red and green lights of the cannery tenders came into sight. After discharging their cargoes of mail, papers and merchandise, they loaded with fish and pulled out again at midnight, heading back to San Pedro.

Fishermen gathered on the barges to dicker for their catches, get their mail and papers, make such purchases as they needed, and do their gossiping. "The talk slid north, and the talk slid south"—the price of fish—weather out on the Flats—how this one had gone down to Tanner on a hunch that albacore were thick down there—how that one was planning to remain at Santa Cruz for the winter crawfishing—how Joe had taken to himself a wife and likely "wouldn't be goin' fishin' no more." It may have been the talk of little folk, but there was something clean and wholesome and windswept about it just the same. As a matter of fact I have heard much worse talk in the lounge rooms of clubs.

But to get back to our fishing. We seemed to be going through a "dry spell." Day after day we combed the sea, piling up a good many miles, but without seeing any fish. We were certain they were there, or reasonably certain. They had been there and it was too soon for them to have left. But during those four or five days if they were there they were "down." We saw lots of sharks, but no swordfish.

[165]

Then, one day about noon, I spotted the two crescent fins of a broadbill. He wasn't a large fish but acted as though he might take a bait. After you have been in this broadbill game long enough you acquire a sort of sixth sense. There are times when you think a fish will bite, even when you first sight him, and there are times when you know he won't. Either way it is surprising how often you are right!

On our third circle we put the bait squarely in front of him. Without any fooling around he boiled the water and went down to it. I saw the tip jerk.

"*He's got it!*" Harry called.

Nothing happened for a few minutes and I went aft.

"He hit all right," Harry said. "Or something did. But I don't feel anything now."

Just as he spoke the fish surfaced far astern of us. Harry reeled in. The bait was unmarked but the leader was kinked about half way up to the middle swivel. It was plain enough that he had whacked it with his bill and gone on—perhaps frightened.

We took after him again and then occurred one of those incidents which have led me to the conviction that a broadbill thinks. I think I have mentioned how they have kept me on the outside of a circle, never letting me head them, reversing when I reversed. That is what happened now. He just kept turning away. Even running full speed I could never head him, never get the bait anywhere near him. He made it very plain that he didn't want to be bothered by us but at the same time had no intention of giving us the satisfaction of driving him down. After a time we gave up and went on our way.

I had just climbed on top the cabin when I caught a glimpse of some thing, or things, black and about half a mile away. Of course I headed for it and, in a very few minutes, again made out two crescent fins cruising nonchalantly along.

Calling Harry, I pointed them out to him and gave him the wheel. That is a very important thing in hunting broadbill. Once you see a fish never take your eyes from him until you are close by. You would be surprised how quickly you can lose them and never find them again.

This one looked bigger than the other. He was swimming high, showing a lot of fin and tail. But he was idling which was none too promising. However, one never can tell in broadbill fishing. Always work them, whether you think they are going to bite or not.

We began to circle, wide at first to prevent scaring him. I don't think we had made more than two circles, and the bait was nowhere near him, when he flirted his tail and sounded, heading just about toward where the bait should be. I threw out the clutch, checked headway, and waited. Harry started peeling off line. Suddenly the rod jerked a couple of times.

"*He's got it!*" he shouted.

There was no doubt about it. This fish wasted no more time going into action than he had going after the bait. Off he went to one side, picking up the slack line in a hurry. As soon as he felt him solid Harry struck hard. Then the reel really began to sing!

Away he went, full speed ahead! It was more like a marlin run, but without the jumps. He must have ripped off three or four hundred feet, then the run stopped and the line went limp. Harry started pumping and reeling like mad.

"He's either off or coming to us!" he said. "But I think he's coming to us. Look out he doesn't cross under the boat!"

Just then a purple shadow showed about fifty feet astern.

"He's coming alongside!" Harry yelled. *"Want to try him?"*

That was a spot to be in! He hadn't been on more than three minutes and here he was coming up within gaffing range. I didn't want to have anything at all to do with him that soon. On the other hand, when you are running a boat it's your job to gaff a fish any chance you get. Harry had recovered all the slack line and had the double line on the reel. In another second the fish would be alongside. Even the swivel was three or four feet out.

I made no attempt to get hold of the leader. I couldn't have held it if I had. Instead, I slid the gaff over the rail and as soon as he was within reach lunged for him just under the dorsal.

But I misjudged his speed sadly. Instead of sinking it where there was some chance of it holding, I got him about two feet forward of the tail.

Right then all hell broke loose! I grabbed the gaff line and made a turn around a bitt. The fish checked and rolled over. Like lightning he recovered and reversed, rushing toward the stern. I checked him again. Again he reversed and raced forward, beating the water with sword and tail. Buckets of water drenched me as I desperately tried to hang on. I could see the big gaff tearing away the pink meat. A broadbill's skin is as fine as silk and there are only two places to gaff them—under the dorsal, or so deep that the gaff comes up around the backbone. Certainly the tail is no place to get them!

The fish was struggling furiously—dashing back and forth, rolling and lunging. Even with the turn around the bitt the line burned my hands. Harry couldn't be of any help, having his hands full with the rod.

For about five minutes—it seemed an hour—the fish and I fought each other. Then the inevitable happened. The gaff pulled out tearing away a good twenty-five pounds as it came. Maddened, he made a tremendous run, faster and further than I ever saw a broadbill go before!

Fortunately when the fish tore lose he was headed forward and away from us. All I had to do was to jump to the clutch and kick her ahead.

He was going too fast and taking too much line. I speeded up. That eased the strain. Then, too, dragging all that heavy line through the water slowed him down. Finally he stopped and started sinking. Harry tightened up and went to work.

It is a sight to see, to watch him working on a fish. Harry spends a good deal of time and a good many thousands of dollars running about the ocean looking for fish. But once he gets hold of one, he wants him in the boat right then and there.

Instead of cruising along as most broadbill do this one started milling precisely like a tuna. Harry was pumping hard but not getting anywhere. When he did recover a few yards generally those, and some more for good measure, would be promptly ripped off. I didn't dare leave the controls as I never knew what the fish would do next. He might suddenly reverse and go astern of us, he might cut underneath, or might head up and across our bows. But it was under the boat he went at last and I got clear of the line by mere inches. Harry had to lean far over the stern, holding his tip under water. But once on the other side, however, he settled down to a hard, lugging fight that steadily took us out to sea.

Harry, who is a very powerful man physically, worked furiously, but for once was forced to take better than he gave. The veins and cords of his neck purpled and swelled. He was getting madder every minute. I could hear him talking to the fish.

[169]

*"Come here! Damn you! You would, would you? I'll show you!
No, by God, you don't! Come here!"*

He swayed back, lifting dangerously high with the rod. Why he
hasn't broken more is beyond me! Once or twice I cautioned him but
he paid no attention. For two solid hours the fish and he had it back
and forth. Then the former began to weaken. No wonder, with
twenty or thirty pounds torn out of him!

He surfaced off to one side, rolling heavily until we could plainly
see the white of his belly. But that doesn't mean anything with a
broadbill. They usually do fight more or less on their side and you
think you have them licked until you find out otherwise.

Harry pumping hard, I edging the boat over, we worked him
close. The swivel came out, hung an instant as the fish lugged, then
shot up toward the tip. I grabbed it, then reached for the middle
swivel. There wasn't any!

That is what comes of being careless when you are fishing. In
the leader box were two fifteen-foot cable leaders with no ring or
swivel to break them. Thoughtlessly I had used one. To make matters worse they were kept in an oil bath and were as slippery as a
greased pig.

Sight of the boat scared the fish. I guess he still remembered that
set-to with the gaff! Anyhow, he flipped his tail and headed up
toward the bow. The leader slipped through my hands like butter. I
tried to hang on when I reached the swivel but by that time he was
going too fast and had too much purchase on me. I had to let go. He
made a big circle out—thank Heaven he didn't try to cross our bows
—and began rolling again about a hundred feet off.

Once again we worked him up until the swivel came out. I had
put on a pair of cotton gloves in the meantime in the hope that they

would be of some help in holding that greasy leader. But they weren't. Just as before, he turned forward and headed toward the bow and I couldn't hold it to save my life. Again he circled out.

Harry was pretty mad by that time and I can't blame him. Here he had brought the fish up to gaff twice—I won't credit him with that first time!—and each time I had bobbled it.

"What th' hell do you want me to do?" he shouted. "Fight him and gaff him both?"

For the third time we brought him alongside. I tried to bunch the leader in my hand. He twisted furiously and again lunged toward the bow. There was but one thing to do—take a long chance. Gripping the leader with both hands I dropped to my knees and clamped it over the cockpit combing. That is about as sure a way to break a leader, or pull out a hook as I know of, but it worked. He turned clear over. Before he could get organized again I got a gaff into him solidly.

Then there were more fireworks. That fish wasn't anywhere near dead, despite the big chunk of meat torn out of him. He lunged and he twisted. He beat the water, the side of the boat, the air, with sword and tail. He lunged vertically out half his length and slashed downward. I'll swear that sword didn't miss my head two inches. I could feel the wind from it as it lashed by! My gaff was pulling out. I yelled to Harry to get another. Handing mine to him I set the second one hard just under and back of his gills. That fixed it although the fish kept on fighting gaffs, water and boat for another twenty minutes.

On the barge's scales he weighed in at 387 pounds—a very good fish. But it was not his weight so much as his tremendous vitality that was so astounding. I don't know a fish that swims that could have been so mangled within three or four minutes after he was hooked, and still put up over three hours of fight that taxed the utmost strength and skill of a great rodman, and then nearly whip two of us on the gaff! Do you?

Harry and I had another session with a tough broadbill but this one, I am convinced, was a very big fish. It was in 1924. Harry had been taken ill and went home for a few days. He called me up and asked me to meet him with the *Angler* at Wilmington. When he came aboard he still looked weak and pale. I suggested that we run straight across to Avalon and wait a day or two before we started fishing again. He didn't say anything, but as we ran out the channel, told me to go alongside Fishermen's Wharf and get some mackerel and barracuda for swordfish bait.

"Never mind," he replied to my objection that he was in no shape to fight a fish. "We'll just run up as far as Point Fermin and then go across. Probably we won't see anything, but the bait will keep on ice all right."

Although I didn't like the idea, there was no use arguing. For once in my life I hoped we wouldn't run across anything. And of course that was just the day when we found one that would bite!

He was a big fellow. Fin and tail were both high and it was an unusually long distance between them. He was just loafing along. I tried to talk Harry out of it but he insisted on having a try at him.

After we had worked him a couple or three times I began to think everything would be all right after all. Each time, before the bait was in front of him, he would race across the line between us and the bait. The fourth time I unconsciously shouted,

"Reel fast!"

Harry skittered the barracuda right in front of his nose.

[172]

"BANG! CRAAASH! RRRRRRRRRRRRRRRRRR!"
He hit with a rush and a roar and was on his way. There was no need
for feeding the bait to him, or letting him swallow leisurely. He
must have hooked himself the first crack and kept right on going.
Harry surged back hard and set the hook.

Well, there we were—hooked on to a big swordfish and a sick
man on the rod!

The fish ran for about two hundred feet, rolled some, then began
to circle us, still on the surface. Harry went after him hammer and
tongs but without fazing him. It was a cold day. A raw wind came
up out of the southeast. Harry had on an overcoat, coat and vest, stiff
shirt, collar and cuffs. Pretty soon he began to shed clothes. First
went the overcoat, then the coat and vest, then the collar and cuffs,
then the shirt—and he was down to undershirt and trousers!

Presently the fish sank and headed out to sea, toward Catalina.
I've often wondered what their idea is, where they think they are
going, for I never hooked one yet between the Breakwater Light and
Point Vincente that didn't do precisely that very same thing.

Weak and sick as he was Harry never let up for a minute. It was
only after two hours had passed that he called for the harness. After
I got him into that heavy canvas contraption he eased up a bit, letting his shoulders take some of the strain while he rested his tired
arms and hands. I don't like a harness and have never used one, holding to the notion that if I can't whip a fish with the arms and hands
God gave me then I'll let him whip me. But that day I was more
than glad to see Harry Adams get into one.

The fish was deep down and fighting a slow, sullen, dogged sort
of fight. Only rarely did he make the usual little short rushes of a
broadbill that tell that he is hurt, or annoyed, or tired. It was as

though he didn't even know that he was hooked—or if he did, didn't care! Three hours and a half had gone by and Harry was growing very tired. His neck was swollen and purple and he was sweating heavily—not the honest sweat that comes with honest labor, but a clammy, unhealthy sort of thing. I soaked a sponge and washed his forehead and held it against the back of his neck.

"That feels pretty good," he said, looking up and trying to grin. There were big circles under his eyes and his face was deeply lined. I didn't like the looks of him.

By two-thirty—we had been on over four hours and a half—the fish had taken us out into mid channel and the sea was kicking up under a freshening westerly. There had been a heavy roll to begin with and now the tops were breaking. I made Harry get out of the chair on the stern deck and down into the cockpit.

There was no change. The fish kept on, cruising steadily toward Catalina and it looked as though he might take us clear across when, without any warning at all, he surfaced and beat the water with sword and tail. Then, and again without any warning, he turned and rushed directly toward us. Harry shouted and tried desperately to keep a tight line on him. Neither of us knew what was going to happen. It looked as though he were charging. We had both been charged by swordfish before and didn't care for it!

About seventy-five feet out he brought up and swung broadside. We could see him plainly in the big seas, turning, rolling, twisting, staring at us with his big yellow eyes. And we saw something else, too. We saw the enormous size of him. When he rolled his back seemed as wide as a skiff!

For about three or four minutes he lay there, then whirled and rushed seaward again, and at the speed of an express train.

[174]

Harry's hard-earned line was vanishing. Unfortunately we were headed in just the opposite direction from the way he was going and there wasn't a chance to turn and follow after. There was only one thing to do—go into reverse and chase him stern first. And that was the *Angler's* one weak point. She would go astern just about as accurately as a tub.

Away we went into that choppy sea, the reverse gear grinding and churning, and every third wave slopping over the stern into Harry's lap. Of course the *Angler* had to veer away from the course the fish was following and that mitigated to a great extent whatever good results might be expected from such a stern chase. But it did seem as though the strain was eased and the line, while it was still running out, wasn't going so fast. Perhaps we were almost holding our own, or perhaps the fish's run had slowed down—it was hard to tell. Nevertheless, eased up or not, he kept on going out to sea and for three-quarters of an hour we kept after him, stern first, and with never a chance at all to get turned around and after him properly.

The reverse gear was making such a racket that I began to wonder how much longer it would hold together when the fish definitely slowed down and stopped. I got headed around bow on to him, then turned my attention to Harry.

He was all in. His face was grey and drawn. The circles under his eyes were deep hollows. The rod slipped in his grasp. He appeared to me to be on the verge of collapse and I begged him to let me cut the line.

"No-No—No," he snarled. "I'm gonna get this damn fish if it kills me!"

Without wasting any further breath in argument he went back to hard pumping. But it was no use. I doubt very much if at any time he regained more than twenty-five feet of line and the fish took that away as though the drag and the arc of the rod were nothing.

At the end of about five and a half hours Harry had to give in. He looked terrible, and I guess he felt worse, when he finally told me that he was all through. It hurt him. It was the first time he had ever given up on a fish. To my mind, though, he had nothing to be ashamed of. To have stayed with such a huge fish for nearly six hours, sick and weak as he was, was little short of incredible and proved beyond any doubt the tremendous vitality, strength and gameness of the man.

Qualified or disqualified, Harry wanted that fish. So did I. We were both morally certain that he was far bigger than anything that had been taken on rod and reel up to that time. Whether fought by one man or two it would be something to land him and show what twenty-four thread line and a sixteen-ounce tip could do. Besides, for the last two hours I had been fairly itching to get hold of that rod. I had an idea in the back of my head that, being perfectly well, and fresh and strong as well, I would make short work of him. It seemed incredible that those five or six hours of hard work Harry had put in on him had failed to leave their mark.

Harry let out some line, then got out of the chair and I took his place. I picked up the slack, set up the drag, braced my feet, and heaved on him.

"RRRRRRR! RRRRRRRR! RRRRRRR! RRRRRR!"

The tip doubled down over the stern and my arms were almost torn from their sockets. I heaved and strained, but not an inch could I gain. On the contrary, he took line from me. As a matter of fact I don't think there was a time during that whole fight that either of us gained an inch through our own efforts. We did get line when the fish came toward us, or when we worked over closer to him, but none through pumping.

Then he took it into his head to make a run of between two and three hundred feet and against the full drag of the reel at that. I might as well have tried to stop a battleship! At last I eased up on the drag and called to Harry.

"It's getting toward dark," I told him, "and we are a good two hours and a half from Avalon. I can't see a chance of getting this fish under six or seven hours, or even then. You're sick and I'm tired. What say we break him off and go home?"

After some argument Harry agreed—but even breaking him loose wasn't as easy as it sounded. I jerked and jerked and jerked until I thought my arms would pull out and still that twenty-four thread held. Don't tell me that seven- or eight-hundred, or even thousand-pound fish can't be taken on it! In the end I was driven to the last resort in such cases. I held the rod straight toward the fish, clamped down with both hands, and Harry kicked the boat ahead with a jerk. That did it and I nearly fell out of my chair when the line finally did snap.

Of course it would be only the wildest guess to attempt to say how much that fish weighed. As I have remarked repeatedly it is one of the trickiest things in the world to try to guess the weight of a fish. On the other hand Harry and I knew broadbill. We knew the various things to look for which give some hint as to the size of them. We had every opportunity to judge this one as he rolled in the swells not seventy-five feet away from us. Both of us are of the honest opinion that he weighed all of eight hundred pounds, perhaps considerably more.

If he had been hooked deep we might have had him. As it was, with the quick rush he had made at the bait and the way he had immediately run off with it, the chances are a hundred to one that he had hooked himself then and there and in the corner of his mouth. I am even more certain that such was the case in view of the fact that never, during those seven hours of hard fighting, had he shown the slightest indication of distress.

And so, we will now leave broadbill. Perhaps, in these chapters, the reader may glimpse something of the strength, the vitality, the individuality of these great fish. There are those who belittle them —who say they are just big sharks, sluggish and sullen, and not to be classed as game fish. I can't agree. True, bluefin tuna will always be the king of game fish with me. But that, I think, is due to their courage, the spectacular nature of their strike, and the fury of their first run. But I also say this: Once hooked, a broadbill will call for more physical strength and endurance on the part of the angler, a greater exercise of wits and judgment, than any other fish that I know. Add to these the fascination of the hunt, the days out on blue water, the uncertainty, and you have as fine a game as could be asked for. And may God forgive those who, in the name of sport, go out and harpoon these magnificent battlers of the deep!

OUT OF THE LOG

A LOG is a sailor's diary. It is the daily record of happenings, the history of the ship's voyage. But this log is different. It is a record of happenings, true enough, but not of a ship, only of a little fishing boat; the matter-of-fact journal of what transpired, what was seen, and what was missed on various days of venture out upon the face of the sea in search of tuna, marlin and broadbill.

Perhaps the phrase "matter-of-fact" is misleading in that it might lead the reader to the fear that what is to come is prosaic. Nothing could be further from the mark. There is more romance and adventure in the thumbed and soiled pages of a fisherman's log than in all the fishing yarns that were ever written. It is only that one must have sufficient vision to read between the lines.

To my mind there is such bald reality in its entries that one is immediately brought close to the surface of the waters, to an intimacy with the everyday happenings that go to make up the game, that one cannot attain through any other means. For myself I would rather read ten pages out of a real log than a hundred of fishing tales. In the latter there is what is known as a "build up." The reader's interest must be held. I don't mean by that that such stories are untrue or exaggerated. Far from it. But full advantage is taken of every incident which will aid in splashing the pages with color. Not that there is any harm in that. God knows there is a wealth of color in the fishing game if one knows how to wield the brush. But the fact remains that these same elaborated incidents are, in nine cases out of ten, taken from the terse sentences of the log and then built up into a story. I'm frank to confess that mine are!

Then there is another thing about a fisherman's log. It plays, or should play, a most important part in the sport of big game fishing. From its record, compared one year against another, checked and cross-checked, comes what little knowledge we possess of the goings and comings, of the whys and wherefores of those mysterious adventurers of the Seven Seas. And its entries likewise offer an almost unlimited field for speculation on matters of which we know nothing.

Many elements enter into the importance of the log. There are, of course, the fish themselves. There are the movements and actions of other and apparently unrelated varieties of fish which, when studied and compared with the movements and actions of their more important brethren, are found to have some sort of mysterious influence upon what the latter are likely to be doing and where they will be doing it. Bird life, too, plays an important rôle. Currents, tides, wind, weather, phases of the moon, water and air temperatures, all have their own particular bearing, and a very vital one, on the subject at hand. And these are but a few of the elements involved. Some are so seemingly remote, so utterly far-fetched, as to cause hesitancy in even mentioning them. For instance—could any reasoning man conceive of a connection between the migrations of butterflies and those of tuna or swordfish? And yet there is every reason to believe that there is such a connection.

After years of such checking, cross-checking and comparing one begins to fit together a sort of sketchy jig-saw puzzle—but with far too many pieces missing. From that puzzle, fragmentary as it may be, it becomes possible to find fish when fish are not supposed to be found.

This business of striving to learn something about fish and their

Alma Overholt, Santa Catalina Island

SEAL ROCKS, SANTA CATALINA ISLAND

movements reminds me very much of the voice of the waters along the hull of one's boat. You lie in your bunk of nights and hear it ripple and whisper along the outer skin. Presently there grows upon you a feeling that it is trying desperately to tell you something—a momentous secret of vast importance. Then, just as this secret is about to be given you, the voice of the waters whispers and dies.

Then again the log of a fisherman pretty accurately portrays the man himself. Sooner or later one glimpses his inmost characteristics, his psychology, his sportsmanship, the days when his digestion is good and when it is bad, if he had been out too late the night before. If you should keep a log, it may not be wise to spread it around too freely!

In the excerpts taken from the log which I have kept over my fishing years there has been no attempt at sequence or order. Immediately succeeding quotations may be years apart, either forward or backward. In other words I am going to skip haphazardly through its pages picking out this or that which happens to strike my fancy or touch some chord of memory. I hope you like it.

May 14.

Avalon 7:30. From Seal Rocks headed toward East End Clemente. Weather foggy, sea smooth, but heavy southwest swell. Wind SE and cold. Current close to Catalina westerly. Very few birds. Put up kite about a mile off Seal Rocks and trolled blind. Wind switched to SW about 11:30 but sky remained overcast. Cold as hell! Had to put overcoat over sweater. No bait surfacing. About 12:30 saw a big hammerhead close by. Enos thought he saw splashes to SW that might have been tuna but nothing showed when we reached where he thought he saw them. Think there are big tuna out in the Clemente Channel if we could only stumble on them. Worked four or five of their surfacing places. The Clemente Channel is a big place to hunt over. Back to dock at 4:05. Lousy day. Dragged a grey dead flying fish over a grey, dead sea all day long under a grey dead sky. To hell with early season fishing!

May 15.

Avalon 7:45. Same sort of day as yesterday. Went out to Far San Diego Bank. Wind SSW. Water looked better than yesterday. Wonder why it is that one bit of water looks fishy and another doesn't? There were more birds and more bait. Also saw half a dozen torpedo sharks. That's always a good sign. Enos said he saw signs of tuna having been feeding but I couldn't. Cruised back and forth until I thought we'd plow a furrow in the sea. Got mad at last after we had passed the same patch of floating kelp about fifty times and told Enos to go back home. Got there about 4:30. At that I think fish are out there. May be feeding at night.

May 16.

Avalon 7:35. Went back to Far San Diego Bank. Fog broke up about 10:30. Water looked summery. Brisk S.W. wind came up about 11:00. Current mainly westerly. Lots of bait, sardines and anchovies—also birds. Some sharks. At 11:30 saw splashes about two miles to the SE. Looked like tuna and had birds over them. By the time we got there they were gone but the birds were still squatting on the water. We trolled back and forth with kite but had no raises. About 12:45 saw more splashes and birds to the southward. Gone when we got there. Worked that spot for an hour without anything. Worked back and forth across the San Diego Banks but saw no fish. Think that what are out there are more to the southward. Back in Avalon at 4:45. Have to go home tomorrow. Told the boys about the tuna and hope somebody gets one tomorrow.

May 17.

Decided to stay another day. Avalon 7:30. Went out to where we saw the fish yesterday. Had plenty of company! Jump, Grey, Goulding, Tad Gray, MacKay and Shorty. Nice day. Cleared early under SW. wind. Plenty of bait and birds and sharks but no fish. Gray saw some but couldn't get into them. They were to the southward of the Banks. Think we all were working too far north. Avalon 4:30. Home tomorrow sure! I think the tuna are working up from Forty Fathom Bank south of San Diego Banks and toward Ben Weston's Flats. Wish I had another day or two to scout for them.

June 24.

Avalon 7:00. Boys on steamer said they saw a big broadbill about 6 miles off Breakwater and on steamer course. Weather fine. High thin overcast with sun shining through. Sea smooth and glassy with gentle NW. roll. Not much current but what there was appeared easterly. Headed toward breakwater about half mile eastward of steamer course. Stayed on top the cabin all the way across. Saw lots of birds squatting on the water and floating stuff. They fooled us three or four times. Thought they were broadbill. About five miles off Breakwater Light changed course to angle toward Pt. Vincente. 10:45 sighted a broadbill swimming high. Looked to be three or four hundred. Active fish. Kept cruising as though hunting. Put out a fresh mackerel and circled him three or four times. Appeared wary and kept turning away. Got the bait in front of him at last and he tore up the water going down to it. Thought sure he would strike, but he didn't. Surfaced off about a hundred yards. Changed bait to barracuda and tried him again. He went down to it and I thought I felt a gentle rap but couldn't be sure. Anyway he surfaced again. The third time we tried him he seemed to get mad and swirled the water with his tail and went down. Lost him for a while then saw him off about a quarter of mile—at least I think it was the same fish. Worked him some more then left him as a bad job. Worked on toward Pt. Vincente and about 5 miles off shore. Sighted another fish about noon but he sounded before we could get anywhere near him. These fish seem timid. Somebody must have been working them. Kept on going. It was a beautiful day. The sea stayed smooth and wind didn't come up until 2:00. Palos Verdes Hills looked like a Maxfield Parrish. Yellow kelp, white surf, chalky cliffs, green gardens leading up to the bare, brown slopes of the hills. Passed three or four party boats. They bristled with rods like a porcupine! Wondered what would happen if they hit albacore. Abeam of Vincente we headed back toward Empire Landing on Catalina. Kite fished across but only had one albacore strike. Missed him. Today was my first shot at broadbill this year and it has every other kind of fishing beat. The whole sea is spread out for you to look at and you don't have to worry about kites or bait whirling, or line twisting. Whether you get a strike or not it's worth all the time put in at it. Back in Avalon 5:15.

June 25.

Took same course across the channel as yesterday. Fine broadbill weather altho not quite so warm as yesterday. Current easterly. Birds and bait all the way across the channel. Caught two albacore on hand lines. Thought they might come in handy as bait. Just west of Horseshoe Kelp spotted two broadbill about a quarter of a mile apart. Both swimming high and loafing. Took after the biggest one first but couldn't get near him as he kept turning away all the time. Finally sounded. Got close enough to him to see a fresh scar on his back. May have been harpooned. Looked around for the second fish. He was still up and tame. Had no trouble getting the bait in front of him but that was all. Tried mackerel, barracuda and albacore but he passed them all up. We ran so close to him I could have scratched his back with the rod! Wind came up about noon and we put up a kite and loafed across to Long Point. Picked up a "little snot" of tuna, as Hooper calls them. 22 lbs. There is no doubt but that there are tuna in the channel. Couldn't help being with all that bait and those birds. Question is whether they are of any size. I doubt it. Back in Avalon at 4:40, sore but satisfied. This broadbill fishing is a grand game but tiring. Think the good weather is over for a while as the wind got pretty stiff by midafternoon.

June 14

Avalon 8:00. Worked close in shore toward Isthmus. Catalina waters are full of small yellowfin tuna between 30 and 50 lbs. It's nice fishing. They take a trolled sardine astern and put up a swell fight on light tackle. They'll take a bait right under the stern and are beautiful sight in the water—sort of lemon yellow. Hit as fast as lightning and make a long surface run. Don't sound until near the end of the fight. Half the time you can see your fish on the surface, fins and tail out. It was a pretty sight. There is nothing bluer than the waters close to Catalina and the green and brown hills lifting up out of them were something to look at. Fishing boats were everywhere and always two or three were hooked on. Fish were as thick as albacore. We got our first one off Goat Harbor. Made a fine long surface run and then circled the boat. Got him in 15 minutes. Picked up four more, all off Empire. That bight was simply full of yellowfin and the flying fish were half crazy. In the air all the time. Our fish weighed 32, 37, 39, 39 and 43 lbs. Didn't bother to note fractional pounds. Everybody brought in fish. These yellowfin on light tackle offer as fine fishing as anybody could ask for—only I wish they were about 20 lbs. bigger.

July 8.

George Romans said he saw lots of tuna about 25 miles off the East End. Zane Grey, Jump, Adams and I went out after them. About 10:30 the fog cleared up under a SW wind and the sea turned a beautiful blue. We were all in sight of each other and it looked as though we were in the bottom of a shallow bowl with the horizons as rim. The twin peaks of San Juan lifted out of the haze a little east of north. We cruised around for about an hour without seeing anything and then everywhere there were tuna—not feeding, just traveling along under the surface and jiggling the water. We got into the school nearest us and Adams had a fine strike. Jump's kite broke off just about the same time and he swung into the trough. Grey was hooked on a minute or two later. Harry worked hard on the fish and got him aboard in about fifteen minutes. A hundred pounder. Put up another kite and soon had another strike. This was a hundred pound fish too. Wherever we looked there were schools of tuna. If you happened to miss one there was another right at hand. The wind was just enough to make a kite work well but not enough to kick up a sea. Hooked our third fish. Another hundred pounder. Both Jump and Grey appeared as busy as we on fish. Ran near Jump once and he blew his whistle three times. I took the rod. Harry put the bait into a school and I had a strike. The fish made a terrific run and then anchored. I worked hard on him and after one solid hour got the swivel out. Told Harry,
"For God's sake get it and hold it! I can't lift another ounce!"

[185]

And I couldn't. The fish was much smaller than the others and later weighed in at 65 lbs. But he gave me a licking even if I did get him. That just goes to show that size doesn't necessarily mean they can fight harder. Harry got his fourth fish, another hundred pounder, and in about 10 minutes. Made me pretty mad to use up an hour on a sixty-five pounder and have him snake in hundred pounders in ten or fifteen minutes. Back to Avalon 5:15. Five fish, 102, 105, 105, 98, and 65. Jump got four and Grey six. There will be a flock of boats out there tomorrow!

July 9.

Avalon 6:30. Got out ahead of all the rest and went to the same ground we covered yesterday. Fleet began to join us and by 11:00 there must have been forty boats! Day much like yesterday but with stronger wind and overcast until after 11:00. Current appeared easterly. Saw no fish. Boats separated and covered a lot of ocean but no one had any luck altho Grey saw tuna splashes far off. I don't think the fish have gone but they certainly weren't up today. Got very sloppy in the afternoon and the run home, four and a half hours, was uncomfortable. Back in Avalon at 5:45.

July 10.

Avalon 6:00. Got out ahead of them all and headed SW. of where we had seen the fish day before yesterday. Think they may be working up Clemente Channel altho they still may be where we found them but down. The easterly current may have had something to do with it. Got out there or thereabouts at 10:45. Fog broke up early and strong SW wind and SW roll. Fished in reaches toward West End Clemente. Saw boats occasionally but too far off to make out who or what they were. Channel grew rougher every hour. At 12:15 had a blind strike of a tuna. Just caught a glimpse of him and he looked pretty big. The rod was lashed and both of us were on top the cabin. Fish missed the bait. Threw over a marker and re-rigged. Trolled back and forth over spot for an hour but raised nothing. Proceeded toward West End Clemente. At 2:30 headed back toward Catalina. Water very rough. Wind so strong we had to run fast to keep up with kite. Think we caught a glimpse of the Clemente Monster. Something big and shiny, like a huge barrel, lifted up out of the sea about a mile and a half away. Lost it right away behind the seas so don't know for sure. It might have been a lump of sea, or even a small boat—but don't think so. Back in Avalon at 6:00. Grey brought in one fish, 72 lbs., that he picked up blind. No one else saw anything. Current was back to westerly again. Think the fish have moved on. Saw very little bait and they have probably left on that account. Broadbill tomorrow.

August 17.

Avalon 7:00. Went out in Clemente Channel. Course SxE from Seal Rocks. Lots of fish are out there. Never knew them to remain so late. Everybody has been bringing them in but us. We've been broadbilling! Adams and I have been experimenting with a rig that should catch two tuna at the same time and on one outfit. As part of leader we use ⅜ Manila rope spliced on to a 3″ ring. From the ring we run a 7′ leader and a 3′. Between the two baits, the ring, and the length of rope, the outfit kicks up a great fuss as it trolls along. Found tuna about 10 miles clear of island. Got into them and hooked two at once! It was certainly a sight to see first one, then a second fish, hit and hook themselves. They threw white water every which way and made a swirl as big as the boat! Only landed one. The long leader broke. My oil slick marker works swell. As soon as a fish strikes I give the bilge pump a couple of turns. That throws enough oil on the water to make a slick. You can see it a mile and a half away. Tuna were everywhere. As soon as we re-rigged hooked two fish again. I never saw anything like those strikes. Apparently the fuss the bait makes maddens the fish and a whole flock of them smash at it at the same time. Again we only landed one. The long leader broke again. It must be that the fish, fighting against each other, whip the rig around and the longer leader, having the most leverage, breaks off. We hooked two fish five times and landed five. Percentage, .500! Each time the 7′ leader broke. But we are both tickled, Adams especially. It has been tough going for the past two or three weeks. He got it into his head that oil on the water spoiled the fishing, and we have spent most of our time running away from oil slicks. With all the tankers coming into Pedro and pumping their bilges there is oil most everywhere. I don't think it makes a damned bit of difference. I've watched closely and seen anchovies and sardines playing in thick oil scum and with clear water near by. I have also seen broadbill go out of clear water into oily water and stay there. I don't see what harm the oil can do them unless it gets into their gills and I think that's unlikely. When a fish surfaces he throws the surface water to either side. Have yet to see any dead fish floating in oily water. But Adams won't listen to me. Now he has something else to amuse him. By using a larger ring I think I can use cable leaders instead of piano wire. Tried them at first on the small ring but they twisted together. If I can make it work without their tangling I think we've got it. Don't like to lose fish with hooks and leaders in them. I think that the piano wire might hold if you let the fish fight themselves, but that won't work with Harry. He wants to get them in right now. Experimented with cable leaders and 6″ ring going home and it worked pretty well. Tomorrow ought to be the day. Our fish weighed 94, 97, 101½, 102, 111. Avalon 5:30.

August 18.

This has been a swell day! Last night somebody told Harry that there were lots of broadbill over between Pt. Fermin and Pt. Vincente and nothing would do but go over there after them. And the Clemente Channel full of hundred pound tuna! I got so damned mad I spoke my mind and we have been snapping at each other all day! I don't care. This has been a tuna year such as we've rarely had and we've spent most of it running away from fish! Between oil and broadbill most of the time our bait has been in the bait box! Ran across on the steamer course to about 5 miles off the Breakwater Light then zig-zagged up coast to Vincente. Didn't see a damned thing but sharks. Don't think there any broadbill there. Half these birds don't know a broadbill from a shark when they see one! Weather was perfect up until 1:30. Fished for tuna back to Empire but nothing doing except a couple of albacore raises. Fourteen tuna, all hundred pounders, out of Clemente Channel today! To hell with it! Put Adams ashore and stayed aboard boat. Don't feel up to listening to the flapjaw in the Club! If he wants fish I don't see why in the hell he doesn't take what God gives him and quit chasing something that isn't there! Anyhow tomorrow we're going after tuna with our doubles rig. Chances are they'll be gone. Their past due now.

[188]

August 19.

Avalon 7:00. Went back to Clemente Channel. Guess I was a good prophet! We covered a lot of ocean but didn't see a thing. The doubles bait worked all right. Wind came up early and by afternoon the channel was white. I rode the crow's nest as long as I could but it got too tough after a while. We blew our chances by not going out there yesterday. No birds or any signs of fish at all. I am pretty sure that they have moved on. Would guess the place to look for them would be off the West End between Catalina and Santa Barbara Islands. Got back to Avalon at 4:30. Too rough to stay out. One fish, small one, brought in.

August 20.

Avalon 7:10. Wanted to try the West End but Adams insisted on going back to the Clemente Channel. Wind SW and strong. Had to use storm kite. Big sea running. Must have been a big blow somewhere outside. Too rough for comfort. No birds, bait or tuna. Boats scattered all over channel but nobody reported any fish. It's the end of tuna all right unless we want to go up toward Santa Barbara or Anacapa. Well it has been a great season. We've taken 22 over a hundred pounds and I don't know how many under without checking. And that in spite of all our crazy running around after broadbill and away from oil slicks. It will be a long time before we have such fishing again. I've a hunch that tuna are on their way out. From now on I think there will be fewer and fewer each year until they finally disappear for a while. We've had them pretty regularly now for 17 years and I think there is a cycle change about due. Back in Avalon 4:45. Broadbill tomorrow.

July 22.

Harry and I have been experimenting with what we call a "Rag Baby." We take a piece of soft wire about as long as a flying fish and weight it to the right weight, then wrap with canvas and paint the canvas red and white. It works on a kite just as good as a flying fish. Left Avalon at 7:15 and went out to Far San Diego Bank. Ran into schools of tuna and put out the Rag Baby without any hook on it. I never knew what fun you could have with

[189]

tuna! As soon as the Rag Baby got into a school they all went for it at once. They'd grab it and drag it under then, when they realized it was artificial, would let go. The kite would jerk it into the air. We'd tied the kite solid with 24 thread. Half a dozen would go into the air after it. They would knock it around, butt it with their noses, grab it and drag it under, let it go again. They just churned the water white! When you put an ordinary bait into a school they either hook on or mash the bait to pulp—and that's the end of that. But this way they keep hitting at it and bouncing it about for fifteen or twenty minutes. To see those big fish split the water, jump fifteen feet into the air, nail the bait in the air and smash back with it, gives you some idea of their speed and power. We put the Rag Baby into five schools and were so excited over the show that we never even thought of putting on a hook. When we did we got one fish, 106 lbs., but it was just an ordinary tuna strike. If anybody wants real fun and the tuna are just an ordinary size that wouldn't mean anything if you did catch them I say by all means rig up a Rag Baby and go out there. You'll see something you never saw before—and you'll learn something about tuna as well. I wouldn't have missed to-day for a hundred dollars.

September 16.

Came up to Santa Cruz yesterday and bucked a stiff NW wind all the way from about 10 miles off Vincente. Had no chance to write up log. Rounded Breakwater Light 9:30 and dropped hook in Smugglers' at 12:30 next morning! Never left wheel for 15 hours. Took plenty of green ones over bows. Beautiful sight at sunset. Sea smother of white. Santa Cruz, Santa Rosa and Anacapa black against fiery red sunset with just a wisp of cloud over them. Thought we would never clear Pt. Mugu. Harry brought aboard some beef for a stew. At 3:30, right during worst of weather, decided he'd go below and cook it. Heard a lot of racket down in the galley and saw Harry sitting on the engine, holding himself with one hand and the stewpot on the stove with the other. Everytime a sea hit us the pot slopped over. He was cussing the stew, the sea and the boat. I pumped about 5 gallons of stew juice out of the bilges this morning. Both of us too tired to think about eating

by the time we got in. From half way down Anacapa Smugglers looked like
a city from the glow of the riding lights of the fishing fleet.

Left Smugglers' this morning about 7:45. Jump is up here. Said there
are lots of broadbill around. Has lost two already. The sea was smooth except for a long swell out of the SW. Sky overcast and wind light S. shifting
to SSW about 10:30. Worked out into the lee water of the islands. Dragged
a flying fish on the chance of a marlin which Jump says are up here. Hooked
a bonito shark at 9:30. Brought him to gaff and killed him. Probably
weighed about 150 lbs. Sighted a broadbill swimming high at 11:00.
Worked him one-half hour but nothing doing. Headed out in general direction of Santa Barbara Island. Weather hazy. 12:30 altered course toward
Gull Islet. Sighted second broadbill at 1:15. Swimming low. Offered him
barracuda. Took it first time. Rolled and threshed on surface for about 15
minutes then sounded, swimming slowly seaward. Harry worked on him
hard and in one and a half hours had him up within about 75 ft. where he
stuck. Made a short run then surfaced again and rolled some more, mixed
with little short rushes. Engine missing. Finally died. Harry turned fish
loose on free reel while I cleaned the ignitors. When we got going again the
fish hadn't taken any line to speak of. Harry worked him hard until he got
the leader out. Fish was surging so heavily I couldn't make a clean gaff and
just ripped off a piece of his skin. Tore loose from me and ran astern about
100 ft. where he rolled and threshed. Harry pulled him over and when he
brought him close up saw a big bonito shark nipping at the gaff gash. Broadbill twisted around and made a long run with the shark after him. Harry
brought him back with the shark still nipping away. Fish made a duck under
the boat with the shark still after him. Nothing we could do could make him
get out of there. He kept Harry running back and forth across the stern in a
sort of Marathon. I poked at the shark with a boat hook but couldn't drive
him away. At last broadbill took out for a patch of floating kelp and fouled
the line in it. Thought he was gone that time but we broke him free. Harry
dragged him over by main strength, the fish was pretty much all in, and the
shark was still worrying him. Somehow or another the broadbill had got the
loose piece of skin I pulled off him wrapped around him and he looked like

a zebra. I got in a couple of shots at the shark which drove him away for few minutes, long enough for me to gaff the broadbill, but he was right back hot after that meat. Harry hammered him on the head with the boathook while I dragged our fish on board, but even then he got two or three good bites out of him. That was the first time I ever knew of a shark tackling a broadbill. The latter seemed afraid of him. I suppose because he was hooked. We finished a bottle of whiskey and threw it overboard. That shark went after that! I got in a couple of good shots at him and think I hit him once. Anyhow he disappeared and we didn't see him again. Fish weighed 387 lbs. on the barge scales and took Harry 4 hr. 22 min. Had fresh swordfish steaks for dinner. All ate on Jump's boat.

September 17.

Smugglers' 8:00. Sea smooth. Sky overcast high fog. Wind light S. shifting later to SSW. Good broadbill weather. Worked out then angled off Gull Islet. Very little bait in sight but lots of birds and sharks. Little after 9:00 it looked as though there were broadbill everywhere! I never saw so many. Counted 46 and we worked 21. If a fish wasn't interested there was always another just a little way off. Most of the fish seemed scary. Think the harpoon boats must have been after them. Never had a real strike all day altho one fish rapped the leader. When you work 21 broadbill in one day and don't get a strike it wears your temper. Harry and I started growling at one another by noon. He claimed I ran the boat wrong and I told him he didn't know what to do when a bait was presented to a fish. Engine was still missing. I had cleaned the ignitors thoroughly the night before and put on new tits but still it missed. Died half a dozen times, always, of course, when we were working a fish. That didn't help matters any! When your fishing goes wrong you blame everything. Got back to Smugglers' at 5:30. Jump will be mad when he hears about all these fish. He had a bad toothache and went down to Pedro last night on the tender. Rob Jump was out fishing but didn't get a strike either. He and I steamed mussels all evening.

Don't think I ever lay in a worse place than Smugglers' of Santa Cruz. All night long it's roll, roll, roll. Looks smooth enough, but there's a nasty little twist that never stops. Doesn't make any difference where you lie. It's interesting up here, though. The albacore are running out on Santa Rosa Flats and bringing as much as $400.00 per ton. There must be all of 300 boats up here of every shape and size. There are four barges from the canneries and Van Camp's floating ice plant. Then there are two floating fuel stations, Standard and Union. Pretty near every race under the sun is represented. There are Americans, Slavonians, Scandinavians, Portuguese, Italians, Mexicans, Japs, Chinks, Russians and negroes. Sounds like a present day Babel when they are all shouting at each other around supper time. The barges are the gathering places. Everybody goes over there and gossips until the cannery tenders get in about 8:00. They return with their loads at midnight. About 2:00 A.M. you hear the fishermen getting under way to go out on the Flats. You could write a good story about it up here right now. Last night one man came in with $175.00 worth of fish! A pretty fair days work! But here's the other side of it. Another boat came in with her rails and false gunwales smashed and all her fish, the two boys said they had a good catch, swept overboard. It's rough work on the Flats. One thing certain, any living you get out of the sea you earn.

September 18.

Smugglers' 7:30. Sea smooth. Sky overcast. Light SW. breeze. Hazy. Worked out from Blue Bank. Saw two broadbill. Worked the biggest one. Went down to it and never showed up again. Went over to the second one and he took the bait the second time it was offered. Harry hooked him solidly and he sounded. Came up in about twenty minutes and after rolling and threshing for a few minutes he jumped clear three or four times. There's something about a broadbill jump that gives me a big thrill. I think it is the sheer power they show when they surge out with that long sword threshing. He wasn't a very big fish. Think he was hooked deep or the leader had fouled him for I saw blood running down out of his gills. Sounded again and the hook pulled out. On him one hour, twenty-two minutes. Wind came up early with fog behind. Kicked up a big sea. Back in Smugglers' at 3:30. Adams has decided he wants to go back to Avalon tomorrow morning. Wish he'd stay put for 15 minutes!

[193]

September 19.

Left Smugglers' 4:15 A.M. Had no charts so had to figure course on mental one. Made it about ExS, ½ S. Should put us about on Long Point, Catalina. Weather very thick. Hard to see bow from wheel. Running past Anacapa couldn't see even loom of island altho heard surf clearly over noise of engine. Harry didn't like it. Never does like fog. His father, who was a ship captain, told him the only thing he feared at sea was fog. Asked me when we ought to pick up Catalina. Told him about 30 seconds before we hit unless the fog lifted. Otherwise about 11:00. Didn't like it and grunted and went below. Fog lifted and broke up in lumps about 10:00. Strong SW wind began to make. Harry came on deck at 11:15 and asked if I'd picked up Catalina yet. Told him I hadn't looked for it. Went up on top cabin and looked ahead. Presently found that one lump of fog didn't blow away. Knew it must be Catalina and went down and told him so. He looked at it, grunted and went below again. Heard him fussing around the galley. Pretty soon he was back with a plate of ham and eggs and potatoes and a cup of hot coffee.

"Here you are, Christopher Columbus!" he said!

Dragged a bait astern and happened to glance at it just as something long and slim came out and lashed down on it. Scared me for a minute. When it came out again saw it was the tail of a thresher shark. Wind increased and lumped up a nasty following sea. *Angler* yawed ninety degrees. Rigged leg of mutton sail and that steadied her. Beautiful sight to see those big seas, all combing, piling down on us from astern. Passed Santa Barbara Island about 15 miles to southward. About 1:30 picked up Ship Rock off Isthmus. We were right on it so my course was just right. Some navigating! Picked up mooring in Avalon at 4:45—12¼ hours—about 90 miles. Had sea legs on me when I went ashore!

September 24.

Left Avalon at 5:30 for Clemente. Took Farnsworth along to run boat. Smooth trip across. Five miles off The Fence had doubles strike from marlin. Harry's fish went to starboard and mine to port. His made a long run and then just laid there. Mine was pretty active so we decided to go after him first. On account of Harry's fish we had to keep the boat still so had to pump my fish in by main strength and awkwardness. Brought the leader out in about 20 minutes but George said he was too lively to gaff. Made a long run, jumping, then sounded. Pumped him back and brought the leader out again. George said he was still too fresh. Made another run and brought him back again. This time Adams ordered George to try for him. Somehow or another he managed to break the leader over the combing. Harry brought his fish in quickly. Can't understand why George didn't try for the fish before. Can't blame him any for not wanting to gaff a green fish, but, at the same time, you don't get doubles very often and when you do they are worth taking a chance on. However, he didn't and I guess that's that. He's a funny fellow and you can't figure him. We re-rigged and started fishing again. A few minutes later had a smashing strike. Made a beautiful run with 34 clean jumps one after another, then sounded. Sulked for a while, then surfaced and made 14 more jumps. Sounded and sulked, mixed up by little rushes back and forth that were hard on the arms. Pumped him up to gaff. Weighed about 175 lbs. Adams' fish about 140 or 150. George kept working toward the island. Pretty soon Adams told him he ought to stay out as there was where we'd picked up the fish and there must be lots of them. George muttered something and spun the boat, heading down the coast. Didn't come down to lunch. About 1:30 Harry hooked a nice fish that put on quite a show, circling the boat and out of the water half the time. Brought him to gaff in 25 minutes. Looked to go over 200. Seems a shame to bring in these fish unless there's some market boat over there we can give them to. Had no more strikes. Anchored in Smugglers' at 4:50.

George was sore and grumpy. Guess he was mad because Adams told him to stay outside. Strange personality. Don't think there's a man living knows as much about fish in these waters than he does. If I could I'd like to hire him by the year. Bet I'd get five times the fishing that the others do.

Never get tired of Smugglers'. Must be its utter desolation. Wind sweeps across the mesa and riffles the cove in little catspaws. Long surges roll in to smash on the beach. Sounds like distant thunder. On the beach are two shacks and a windmill. Instead of making it look inhabited they only make it more lonely. This evening a man came down to the beach and stood looking at us. Probably a sheep herder. Pyramid Head shows five distinct beach lines. I've been told that on the mesa, back of Pyramid Head, is what appears to be an altar made of rocks laid in geometrical patterns. If so must antedate Indians the Spaniards found by a long, long time. Think I'll try and find it some time. Two Jap jig boats are anchored nearby, their skippers squatting in the sterns and gossiping. Can hear the staccato of their talk as I write. George is up forward studying the sky.

September 25.

Left Smugglers' 7:15. Worked out a little then worked toward China Point. Overcast sky and light SE wind with heavy ground swell. Inspiring sight to see the big seas smash on the black, jagged rocks of China Pt. God help the boat that goes ashore there. Can see ribs of purse seiner that smashed up there last year. Turned and worked back across Smugglers' and up North side of island. George was still grumpy so Harry told me to go up and see if I could find what was the matter. Finally got it out of him. Just as I thought he was mad because Harry told him to stay outside yesterday. Said he figured he was hired to find fish and if he wasn't permitted to use his own methods there was no sense in hiring him. Said he had wanted to go in shore and study the kelp and the rock bass and perch. Could figure from these where the tuna and marlin were and what they were doing. Maybe so, I don't know. I sympathized with him but pointed out that since we had been getting strikes out there he couldn't blame Harry for wanting to stay. Then he told me that there were only marlin there and he thought there were big yellowfin tuna somewhere around Clemente. That explained it. He'd rather catch one tuna than twenty marlin. Anyhow he calmed down and got cheerful for him. I went below for a nap about 11:30 and was awakened by the boat running full speed. Ran up on deck and found that we were circling full speed ahead. Sea was like glass and there wasn't a sign of anything. George claimed he'd seen signs of tuna deep down. Maybe so. Anyhow we didn't raise anything. Kept on up island. At 2:30 Harry had a marlin strike but fish threw hook at second jump. Worked back from Long Point, in and off shore.

Ran in off Ghost Rock at 4:00 and dropped for groupers and sand dabs for supper. Three drops gave us a fine mess. Anchored behind The Fish Hook. Another lonesome place. Just a little cove behind a jagged reef. Room for about two boats. High cliffs seem to overhang. At night you hear the surf on the reef, sea lions once in a while and goats bleating from the cliffs overhead. Best anchorage on island in all except Easterly weather. Sea stayed glassy all day until about 4:30 when evening easterly came up. Never saw it so calm at Clemente. What current there was seemed mostly westerly. Avalon tomorrow.

September 25.

Fished up to The Fence, then put up kite and headed across to Catalina. Wind came up early and kicked up lumpy sea. Saw nothing all the way across. Picked up mooring at 3:30. Still can't see why George didn't gaff that marlin when we had doubles on.

July 9.

Avalon 6:45. High fog, smooth sea, wind light S.E. shifting to WSW about 11:00. Current westerly. Headed NNE toward Newport. About 14 miles out passed under stern of Luckenbach freighter inbound on Panama course. Picked up a bunch of bananas thrown overboard. Some were all right. Followed shark. Thought he was a broadbill. Picked up Huntington Beach oil wells about 10:15. Saw tuna splashes to eastward toward Red Bank. Ran over and found sea alive with them—all big fish. Acted different from any I'd ever seen before. Popped up in little bunches. Just a flurry of half a dozen splashes and they'd be gone. Trolled with kite back and forth and all through area where they were working and never had a strike. The sea under us must have been packed with them. Can't understand why we got no raises. Of course tried to get into surfacing fish but always missed. Sometimes only by a few feet but even then we raised nothing. No bait on surface to indicate where fish might be expected to pop up. Worked in them until about 2:30 when they disappeared. On way home picked up one blind. 114 lbs. This being my birthday guess it was meant as a present! Can't figure out this change in the way tuna are working. No apparent difference in sea, weather or current conditions. Asked Farnsworth about it but he only grinned and said— "You're liable to see a lot of difference from now on." Maybe so. My guess is that there are so many fishing boats out of Pedro that the fish have changed their habits. Maybe it's one of Nature's protective provisions. One thing, it will make it tough on purse seiners if they keep it up. Ha! Ha! Back in Avalon at 5:35. Ours the only fish today.

July 10.

Avalon 6:30. Headed back for where we found tuna yesterday. Still overcast with light SE wind shifting to SSW about 11:00. Fish still there and acting as they did yesterday. Four or five purse seiners hanging around. Tickled us to see them with their nets out and no fish! It's a half day job to put out a net and take it in! They've been getting away with murder. Nets are 2500 ft. long and 250 deep. One haul will take more fish than all the hook and line fishermen in the world could get. Ninety per cent. of them are aliens, Slavonians, and yet we let them come in here and destroy a great natural resource. Damn the politicians! After running all around I finally got into one bunch surfacing and Harry hooked a fish right off. That settles it. If you get into them you get a fish. If you don't you're out of luck. Weighed 112 lbs. and took him 25 minutes. Seemed to me the fish was faster and lugged harder than tuna normally do. Maybe just imagination— but 25 minutes is a long time for Harry to take on a fish that size. While we were hooked on another bunch popped up about fifty feet away. They made the water boil, but there was no sign whatever of any bait. Got into another bunch and Harry hooked his second one. Put up same sort of fight as the first and took him 23 min. Weighed 113½ lbs.

September 16.

Left Mosquito at 7:00. Overcast, no wind, light roll coming down coast. Worked up toward Long Point and about a mile and a half off shore. I was sitting on top the cabin and Roy was below doing something. Rod lashed to chair. Off White Rock saw something big and black out of the corner of my eye and to seaward. Turned, and there it was—the Clemente Monster! Nearly fell off cabin. Yelled to Roy to head for it and clapped my glasses on it. It's hard to describe just what I saw. The thing lifted out of the water about 20 ft. I should say and looked to be 8 or 10 feet thick. A sort of huge barrel, or tree trunk, with a kind of lizard like head. On each side the head, which I gathered was lowered, as I didn't see any mouth, there were two huge eyes. They must have been sixteen or eighteen inches across and were round and bulging. Dead and expressionless. The head was turning slowly. I got the impression of coarse reddish hair, or bristles, on the columnar part that was in sight. It was about ¼ of a mile off when I sighted it and I think my glasses being 7-power should have brought it up to within perhaps 200 yards of us. It is only an hour ago that we saw this thing and I am writing this carefully and while all details are fresh in my mind. Roy stuck his head through the hatch and let out a sort of little squawk when he saw it. We both knew what it was because we had both heard of it and talked to people who had seen it and I saw it once a long way off. The description given by others checked with the thing I was looking at. All of them had described it as a thick body surmounted by a reptilian head and with God awful eyes. Certain the eyes I was looking at were God awful enough. I never want to look at anything like them again! The head was turning, sort of pivoting. It appeared to see us and stopped, staring at us for perhaps a minute, perhaps more. Then it started to sink. There was no convulsive movement or anything like that. It just sank down slowly and deliberately much as a whale's fluke's sink when it up ends and sounds. When it disappeared there wasn't any discernible ripple or swirl. It just went under. Looking back and taking stock of things I remember another thing. The little roll coming down the coast *broke* against it! That gives some hint of the size of it. We've been lying to for the last hour hoping that it would come up again. Roy and I have been trying to figure out what in the name of God the thing is. Certainly it's no known living creature. The thing looked very much like the models I have seen of brontosaurs (I hope I'm spelling that right!) that I've seen in museums. Roy is plain scared and I don't mind saying I'm not so happy as I might be. As I write this I am sitting on the cockpit bench and I find myself glancing overside all the time. Still, I wish it would come up and let me have another look at it. I don't know how long it was up but would guess at about two minutes. Roy says five, but I don't think so. I know we didn't seem to get appreciably nearer to it. After it was all over I realized I had a kodak on board! But I don't suppose it would have shown anything but something black sticking up out of the water. One thing, visibility was good. The island behind us stood out in clear detail and the horizon edge was sharp. So there was no haze to distort what we saw. I don't know what the thing is—and don't think anybody else does. But I know now that there is something out there that is unknown and unclassified. Probably it is something that has come down out of prehistoric times. I am certain the thing is warm blooded and has to surface to breathe. There were no signs of gills that I could see. Roy's impressions of it coincide with mine—except that he says it was fifty feet high! That's nonsense! I think it lifted up 20 ft.—but it might have been less. It might have been 6 ft. thick and not 10. But the neck, or body, or whatever it was we saw was apparently perfectly round—and the head was flattened and reptilian. And nobody can laugh away those eyes.

Later: We got the horse laugh in camp tonight but the fact remains that we saw something that isn't! I've wracked my brains to see if I've overlooked anything but if I have I can't think of it. Incidentally we caught one marlin —about 175 lbs. Put up a nice fight with about 30 jumps. Somehow or another, though, my mind isn't on fishing today! What in the hell was that thing!

July 6.

Avalon 7:30. Worked out over San Diego Bank then angled off into Catalina Channel. Wind SW in Clemente Channel, WNW in Catalina. Bought a new 4–0 Vom Hofe reel last night and am using it with light tackle outfit. Kite up. At 10:45 had terrific tuna strike. Didn't see the fish but he made the longest run I've ever seen. Had on 1200 ft. new 9-thread line and 300 ft. of old as filler. Took out all the new and about 100 ft. of old! Doesn't seem possible. Fortunately he ran straight and Walker took after him. Expected the line to break every minute but it didn't and I got most of it back and over the fish. Think that Walker deserves most of the credit. Fish surfaced and started circling us. Could see his back and fins about 300 ft. off.

Walker swore he would be 100. I could work him up to about 100 ft. from us and there he'd stick, turn, and make another run. Was scared to put too much strain on him as I don't know much about this light tackle on big fish. Line tested 22 lbs. this morning but that's not much on a hundred pound fish. After about 1½ hrs. the fish sounded and started tuna milling. Worked on him hard and pumped him up within sight where he stuck again. Looked badly whipped and was half on side but still had too much strength for me to risk on light tackle. Kept after him and in another half hour had him pretty close. Walker had the gaff ready and we thought a couple of minutes more would bring the swivel out. I guess I lifted a little too hard for the hook pulled out. The fish laid there for two or three minutes then sounded. I don't know if he weighed 100 lbs. but will say he looked close to it. One thing certain he would have been the biggest tuna taken on light tackle to date. That was a cinch. On him 3 hrs. and 45 min. Back in Avalon 4:30.

* * * * * * *

So, there they are, a hit-and-miss selection of extracts from a fisherman's log. They cover a good many years and every one of them carries with it its particular memory. Be kind enough to forgive grammar, abbreviations, and so forth. After all they are part of the picture. Most often it was written up at night after the day's fishing and when I was dog tired.

As a matter of fact I think I have experienced more emotions in pawing through the pages of these log books than anyone could possibly experience in reading the extracts. A million memories come rushing upon me in a veritable tidal wave. Each page is filled with them. Some of the pages are smeared with oil, some with plain dirt, and some with blood. Out of them have peered the faces of old friends long ago embarked upon the long traverse to the "Happy Fishing Banks." I have seen the ghosts of little white boats, long ago disappeared from off the face of the sea. Again I have felt the sting of wind and sun and salt—seen the shifting blues, purples, violets, mauves and rose of the heaving, restless waters. As I bring the chapter to its end my heart is somewhat sad. Those were grand days— and they are gone forever. Adiós, old friends, and old days!

DEAD WATER

MOST everyone who has gone down to the sea knows the lanes of dead water which lie between the current drifts and stretch their winding ways for miles and miles. To those of us who have ventured out in little ships—whose lives have been spent very close to the tumbling surface of the sea—these lanes of dead water are of extraordinary interest. For hours on end we have worked along them, weaving back and forth across their paths. We have seen, and studied, the varied accumulation of flotsam and jetsam that has ultimately found a resting place there, tossed for the moment aside into these eddies of the currents. From them we have learned something of what is going on under the blue, sphinx-like face of the sea. We have watched the deep water minnows sheltering under a patch of floating kelp—the queer-shaped, wobble-finned sunfish—little blue sharks—strange varieties of organic life which we, in our ignorance are unable to name or classify, but which, if we only knew how to read them, tell their story of the sea, of its creatures and what they are doing, or likely to be doing.

And, as for the other inanimate odds and ends that gather there to rest awhile until some vagrant current eddy picks them up and carries them forward upon their endless journey back and forth across the waters, their diversity is unbelievable.

I like these sinuous lanes of dead water. I like to loaf along them, observing the teeming marine life, the multitudinous drifting things. And because I like them, and because there is to be found along them almost every conceivable object, animate or inanimate, I have the fancy to entitle this "Dead Water."

After all, that is what it is. It is the dead water between the current drifts of memory. In it all sorts of things bob aimlessly about— half forgotten scenes and faces—stories—incidents—adventures— the Lord knows what. I have thrust my dip net into it and hauled forth this and that. And among my haul are these.

It was the summer of 1923. I was fishing with Harry Adams out of his *Angler*. We were hunting broadbill, leaving Avalon early each morning and cruising the twenty odd miles across to the main-land side. This particular morning we started just a little behind Zane Grey in his *Gladiator* and followed the steamer course toward San Pedro. Grey was a little to westward and bearing further away as we crossed the channel.

When we were well clear of Long Point, probably five or six miles, Harry, who was sitting on top the cabin, called to me to come up. He was considerably excited.

"Look over there toward Grey," he said, pointing. "What the hell's going on there?"

I could just see the *Gladiator* on the horizon. She appeared to be tearing around in circles in the midst of a tremendous commotion— great flashing splashes.

"Big tuna!" I exclaimed excitedly, and swung toward the fuss.

"Tuna, hell!" Harry snorted. "You never saw tuna that big, and if they are they're trying to escape with their lives! You'd never get a strike out of 'em!"

Grey was tearing around in big circles. Through the glasses I could see people crowded at every point of vantage. Enormous black shapes leaped high into the air and crashed back with terrific splashes. Harry was right. These were no tuna.

MARLIN LUNGING

TIRED MARLIN SURFACING

It took some time for the slow *Angler* to reach the scene and by the time she did the show was almost over. But even then it was something to remember as long as one lived.

A big school of killer whales—Orca gladiator—had rounded up a school of porpoises. Later we learned that they had been following them for days. The porpoises were utterly exhausted. One could readily picture the horrors of that chase. The porpoises rushing madly up the channel. The great killers following inexorably, raiding into them, picking up those that fell by the wayside. Now, the chase was ended. The poor little fellows had come to the end of the trail. The killers had closed in. Followed, the slaughter!

A patch of about ten acres was one mass of orcas, leaping porpoises, chunks of meat and bloody foam. Thousands of sea birds fought screaming over the raw meat. Porpoises leaped into the air—killers after them. One jumped a full twenty feet within ten feet of us. Out after him came a sinister black shape that caught him in mid air, shook him as a terrier does a rat, and tore him to pieces before our very eyes.

On board the *Gladiator* everyone was on deck shouting and yelling like Indians. Cameras clicked and ground. Grey took some wonderful pictures of that show. They are in his *Tales of Swordfish and Tuna*. Few human beings have been given the opportunity to have brought before their eyes the merciless struggle that forever wages beneath the surface of the waters. To be able to preserve its record in pictures is a priceless gift.

A frantic, harried porpoise took refuge under our bilges. Half a dozen orca rushed after him. When they hit us we rocked as though in a collision. Harry got out the big swordfish gaff—I guess with the vague idea of gaffing one of them.

[205]

"Don't do that, you damned fool!" I yelled.

I wonder what would have happened if he had jabbed it in. Later Grey told me that they all yelled, "Good-bye, Harry!"

There was a sudden furious flurry of leaping porpoises and killers—and the sea settled down to its former peacefulness. I climbed down from the cabin and wiped the sweat out of my eyes. Harry looked at me and I at him. The *Gladiator* pulled up alongside.

"I thought you were gone, Harry!" Grey shouted over. "Did you think you could gaff one of those things? Did you ever see anything like it in your life?"

We hadn't and I doubt if many others have. I know I shall not forget it.

The orca gladiator, or killer whale, is one of the few vicious things—at least that we know of—in the sea. They hunt in packs and are fiercely voracious. Most fishermen fear them. I had always been warned to give them a wide berth, especially if there happened to be cows with calves. I have seen them pick seals off the rocks. They will come two-thirds their length out of the water and drag them off, tearing them to pieces then and there. During one of the British Antarctic Expeditions, I forget whether Shackleton's or Scott's, ponies were taken along with the idea of using them to drag the sledges. Base was established at the edge of the Ice Barrier and the ponies were taken out upon floes for exercise. Those waters swarm with orca. Quickly they sensed the proximity of flesh. In great herds they gathered about the floes, trying to climb upon them, reaching hungrily for the frightened animals. This failing, they gathered under the floe, rolling up and tilting it so dangerously that it was necessary to rush the ponies to safety.

Orca are sometimes called blackfish, but they are quite different

[206]

in appearance from the blackfish that I know. The latter are square nosed, with low dorsal fins, and unmarked. The orca, on the contrary, have more pointed heads, very high dorsals, and greyish stripes running from behind the dorsal down to the belly. Their mouths, furthermore, are filled with long, murderous teeth. Both, of course, are mammals, of the whale family.

Orca gained their name of killer whales from their habit of attacking whales. So far as I know I never have seen one do it—although once I saw a terrific commotion out on the horizon that might have been such a battle. I am told, however, by those who ought to know, that they do not tear a whale to pieces. Instead they are apparently interested only in the tongue, attacking the big creature, worrying him until they can get their heads inside his mouth and tearing the tongue out.

The orca gladiator is a vicious, voracious creature and one that should be left strictly alone.

There have been some queer characters among the famous Avalon boatmen. Taking them by and large I hold them in the highest respect. I am convinced that there isn't enough money in the world to persuade one of those boys to come and lie about a fish. They take their work seriously—and it is hard work. Day after day they go out upon rough water, dealing with all sorts and types. Half their customers don't know the first principles of angling, but are quick to find fault with the boatman if a fish is lost, or if none is found. Hooked on to a fish they must handle the boat skillfully, coolly—more so if the angler is inexperienced. It is my opinion that the credit for successfully taking a big fish goes sixty per cent to the boatman and forty per cent to the angler. There will be those who disagree in this! Their boats must be clean. Their tackle must be of the best—no small investment in itself. They must bring in fish if they are to secure parties. I have no doubt that there have been numberless times when temptation has been offered them, but I don't know of a single instance when any of them has brought in a disqualified fish and claimed it was taken fairly. They receive from $20.00 to $25.00 a day for their services. This includes everything but lunch and bait. If you haven't your own tackle they have as good gear as you can find in any Tuna Club locker. Their season is a scant three months with a little off and on fishing during the spring. Out of what they earn they must live, keep their boats smart and seaworthy, and their tackle up to date and in good order. To the best of my knowledge none of them has as yet retired upon his earnings. I think they are all right. They have given me a lot of pleasure and I'm for them.

I have read a lot of fishing books. Far too few of them see fit to give any credit to the boatman. Big game angling was cradled at Santa Catalina Island. To my mind boatmen have played a greater part in making the game what it is today than have the anglers. Now these boatmen are fading out of the picture. Time is thinning their ranks. There is but a handful of the old timers left. Twenty years ago there were probably thirty of their lockers along the Avalon Pleasure Pier. Today I doubt that there are ten. Soon these ten will be empty and the men who picked up big game fishing in its infancy, who worked hard, who experimented and profited by mistakes, who fought wind and sun and rough water, who suffered in silence the vagaries of their employers, will be gone from among us. They are always trying and they are sportsmen—and a sportsman is a sportsman whether he is holding a rod, running a boat, or digging a ditch.

Forgive this little tribute. They have earned it. God bless them all!

Of all the characters among the Catalina boatmen I think Enos Vera is the most lovable. An Azores Portuguese, Enos has fishing sense bred into the very bone of him. First, his "lil *Pirate*," and later, his *Carrie* are part and parcel of Avalon Bay and of Catalina fishing. Around about him has grown up a wealth of yarns, humorous and philosophical. You can tell them to Enos' face. He doesn't mind. Just laughs a deprecating, gold-toothed laugh.

"Oh, everybody she make a th' fun o' Enos!" he says deprecatingly. "Enos don' care. He catch a da feesh. He don' mind da laugh."

Once he was over at San Clemente with Jump who had as guest a man whose first name was Jack. The letter "J" is impossible for Enos; he invariably makes it a "Y," calling this man "Mis' Yack."

"Mis' Yack" was having trouble hooking marlin. There were lots of them there but he missed strike after strike. Enos finally lost patience and told him he didn't know *how* to strike a swordfish.

"Listen, you blankety blank Dago," the other roared, nettled at the criticism, "did you ever catch a swordfish?"

"No, Mis' Yack," Enos answered grinning his gold-toothed grin, "I never catch no swordfish. An' beside, I no Dago, I Portugee!"

At last "Mis' Yack" connected, landing his fish. Naturally he was well pleased, and equally naturally he couldn't help rubbing it in a little.

"There!" he exclaimed triumphantly, throwing down his rod and pointing to the fish. "That's a swordfish, isn't it? And I caught it, didn't I?"

"Yes, Mis' Yack, that swordfish, all right, and you catch she, all right." Enos countered. "But, Mis' Yack, that littles' swordfish I ever see!"

Another time there were a lot of forty- to fifty-pound yellowfin tuna around Catalina. Everybody was getting them but Enos. Day after day his angler missed strikes and lost fish. Day after day Enos' spirits fell lower. Then one day Jump came up to him off Empire Landing. Enos waved frantically and Jump, thinking he might be in some trouble, ran over to him.

"Come 'ere, Mis' Yump!" he started shouting when Jump was in earshot. "You come 'ere! I got a lot o' bait I wan' give you!"

By this time the two boats were side by side and Enos began throwing buckets full of sardines into Jump's.

"This good bait, Mis' Yump!" he declared. "I want you should have him. You take 'em—use 'em! You get lot o' tunny!"

"Hey, wait a minute!" Jump protested. "Don't do that! I've got plenty of bait! There's lots of fish around! Your man'll need it!"

Enos shook his head. "Ha! Ha!" Enos retorted. "You don' know, Mis' Yump! He don' need no bait! This feller here he can't catch no fish nohow!" Tapping his dejected angler on the shoulder he asked him: "Mister, is you ain't got more luck in your biz than you got in your fish, how you mak' 'nough money to go fish?"

There might be something in that!

Another time I was out with him in the *Pirate*, a little twenty-two foot open launch. We were about ten miles off the East End. About noon Enos began running up forward, unscrewing the cap of the gasoline intake, and sticking a rod down into the tank. After he had done this four or five times I grew uneasy.

"What in the hell are you doing, Enos?" I demanded.

"Oh, I jes' forget gas this morning an' I like know how much we got left!"

That was a fine piece of news, way out there where we were!

"All right! How much you got?" I asked. "Enough to get home?"

"Oh yes—I got 'nough to get home all right."

"All right! Turn around and let's get back there!"

He obeyed and we ran along for three or four miles when he came upon a broadbill. Enos was tickled to death—all smiles and rubbing his hands.

"There broadbill!" he exclaimed. "Now we get broadbill! We take 'im home!"

I looked at him aghast. "Get hell!" I snorted. "How are we going to fight a broadbill for maybe four or five hours when we've only enough gas to get home on?"

That didn't faze Enos. "Oh, that all right," he came back. "You hook 'im. Then I shut off engine an' row lil *Pirate*. Pret' soon you get 'im, then Enos start engine an' we go home!"

Simple enough, but we didn't try it!

Good old Enos! I think a lot of him. Many are the happy days we have spent together out on the blue sea; many are the good fish we've taken—and many more are the good fish we've lost. Enos will always be a living part of my memories of fishing. I hope he never goes the way of all flesh. Rather, I hope, the gods of fishermen, who must be very kindly and very understanding, will, when his days have run their appointed course, gently pick him up and speed him down the long traverse to the Happy Fishing Banks. There he will meet old friends and patrons. There he will never lack for parties on summer seas where the sun, "she always shines, and the feesh, she are always big feesh." A lot of good fellows will shout: "Hi, there, Enos!" when they see him pulling shoreward to that golden sand.

Then there was Monty Foster. Monty has embarked upon the long traverse. But he was a character, too. He was an Englishman, with all the dry, unexpected humor of his people. They used to tell a lot of stories on Monty, but this one, I think, is priceless.

He was over at San Clemente after marlin. His angler was having the same difficulties all of us have experienced. He was missing strikes. Monty kept pounding at him to let the fish run, but the man didn't seem able to resist clamping down as soon as he felt anything.

We were sitting around the supper table at Mosquito Harbor one night and Monty was complaining bitterly about his luck.

"I say, old chap," he suddenly said to his man, "I'll tell you what to do. Tomorrow, when you get a strike, give a yell, then let him run until I tell you to soak him!"

The following night they came in empty-handed and both out of temper. It seems this is what had happened. The man had had a strike and shouted. Monty, who was on top the cabin reading a book, something he always did, didn't hear him. The line raced out faster and faster. Again he called and again Monty failed to hear him. At last he stood up and yelled:

"Hey there, Cap! I've got a fish on! Shall I strike him?"

Monty finished his paragraph, dog-eared the page, and glanced down at the reel. There was about two hundred feet left!

"Suit yourself!" he replied—and went back to his reading!

There was Shorty Stoughton and his dog Pard. Pard always

went out fishing with his master, curling up in the bow and sleeping peacefully until tuna were near. Then he would wake up and bark his head off. We always suspected that Pard saw fish before Shorty did! Give him five cents and he would take it in his mouth, go down the street to the butcher shop, lay it on the counter and wait patiently until he got his piece of bologna. Then Shorty died. Pard was heartbroken. Day after day he would sit on the beach, looking out to sea, and whimpering. It wasn't long before he died, too. Nobody can tell me those two aren't together again!

Old Hugo! I never did know his last name. He was a Norwegian sailor who forsook the sea to fish, then forsook fishing to pull one of those glass-bottom rowboats that made Catalina's marine gardens famous. It is still the best way to see them. But times have changed. Now they have big, paddle-wheel, Diesel-driven glass-bottom boats carrying two or three hundred passengers, hurrying in and out from the pier amid the din of whistles and the ballyhoo of barkers. They soon drove the little rowboats out of business. But Hugo was the last to give up the ship. Day after day he would hang around the Pleasure Pier in his awning-topped boat as the big boats were loading.

"Ha-ha-ha!" Upward floated his chant. "Th' Wreegly glass bottom power boat! She smoke, an' steenk, an' blow th' veestle! Ha-ha-ha!"

What a world of bitterness was in that chant—and what helpless indignation at being driven from an honest livelihood. And, oh, but didn't it infuriate the brass-buttoned, gold-striped, bejeweled barkers!

Why, I could go on for hours and hours digging back into the past, dipping out of the dead waters of memory this and that anecdote, or relating the doings of those old time Avalon boatmen and anglers.

There was the case of Ray Millsap, who showed, I think, one of the finest examples of quick thinking, of presence of mind in the face of deadly danger, that I have ever heard of.

Millsap used to spend part of his time albacore fishing. That meant starting out about two o'clock in the morning and fishing until around noon. He fished alone. One morning when it was still dark he fell overboard about fifteen miles off the East End of Catalina. There was a spot to be in! He was a good enough swimmer, but not good enough to swim any fifteen miles. His boat kept on going in great circles and without any chance at all of his getting to it. Most of us would have struck out desperately for the island and used up all our strength in the first mile. But not Millsap! After the first panic he took quick stock of his situation and got rid of his pants and shoes. In another hour it would be broad daylight. There were a great many boats fishing those waters. The water was reasonably warm and there was no danger from exposure for some time. Making himself as comfortable as possible he paddled along just enough to keep himself afloat. When daylight came he started splashing the water with hands and feet. In due time another boat saw the splashes, thought they were fish, came over and picked him up. They caught up with his launch and he climbed aboard and went on with his fishing! Clever and nervy, wasn't it?

I don't seem able to get away from those old time Avalon boat-

[214]

men. Their faces pass in endless procession in front of me. Jim Gardner, Mexican Joe, Joe Adargo, George Farnsworth, George Johnson, Harry Elms, Quigley, Tad Gray, Monty Foster, Chappie, Nick, Roy Staples, Percy Neale, Dan Danielson, Yellowtail Johnnie, Smithy Warren, Sam Goulding, Hugh MacKay, Enos Vera, Sid Boestler, the Markham boys, Joe and Chet, Kent Walker, Shorty Stoughton, Alex Adargo, Jim Bates, Parker Pence, Harry Warner, Lee O'Leary, Newberry and all the rest whose names I can't, at the moment, recall. I wish I could deal with each one of them, but the particular chip which is theirs floating and bobbing in the dead waters of memory seems to elude me. But dead, or alive, if any of you should happen to read these pages, surely you will know by now how much I think of you.

Were you ever charged by a rampaging, angry broadbill swordfish? I was—and I didn't like it! And I know three or four others who were—and they didn't like it either.

It happened this way. I had hooked on to a broadbill, a pretty good sized fish, and fought him for four or five hours. Two or three times during the fight he had surfaced and lunged out. Twice he started to swim toward the boat then apparently thought better of it. After a while he went down and stayed there. But he didn't travel as most of those fish do. Instead he just milled around slowly, rolling heavily. We couldn't get from directly over him to save our souls. That sort is hard to fight. The line goes straight down over the stern and the downdrag is terrific. I got tired of it after a while and started surging on him, thinking that that might wake him up. It did, and with a vengeance! Up he came, broaching two hundred feet off to one side, rolling and beating the water with his sword.

All of a sudden he headed directly for us, half out of the water, jaws wide, broadsword waving angrily. My boatman yelled and ducked down into the cabin. I yelled too, but had nowhere to duck. Straight for us he came, just skittering along the surface, and so fast that I couldn't pick up the slack. Just before he hit us—I don't think he was ten feet away—he dove under the boat, broke water on the other side and ran off a little way.

Quick as a flash he whirled and charged us again, going through the same proceeding. Again he whirled and charged. Cap tried to get away from him but he followed us, changing his course when we did. There wasn't the shadow of a doubt but that he was after us. For ten or fifteen minutes—it seemed like ten or fifteen hours!—he kept up these tactics then sounded again. Ultimately the line broke and for once I was glad of it!

When it was over both of us were white and shaking and drenched with water from his leaps close by. Why he didn't hit us, I don't know. Perhaps the churning propeller scared him off, perhaps it was the boat. If he had hit us, I don't know what would have happened. Of course, if he had rammed us with his sword, the impact would probably have knocked him out or killed him. But it would have left us with a splintered hole in our hull. What worried me most was the likelihood of his leaping aboard. That would have been a bad mess. It is not hard to imagine what it would be like with three or four hundred pounds of maddened swordfish lashing around the little cockpit of a boat. I know that while the show was going on I vaguely made up my mind that, should he come aboard, I would take to the water! That was the safest place I could think of with that fish in the cockpit.

And now I come to the question as to whether or not swordfishing is dangerous. I don't think it is as a general thing, but there is always an element of potential danger involved. Both broadbill and marlin are very large fish. They are equipped with a dangerous weapon. Broadbill *do* charge boats. Marlin, when hooked, go raving crazy, in and out of the water, here, there and everywhere, so fast it is hard to count their jumps. A maddened marlin would just as soon jump into a boat as not, if it happened to be in his path. The fact that, so far as I know, one has never done it doesn't mean anything. I've had them miss me by not more than four or five feet. One of these days a crazed marlin, or an infuriated broadbill, is going to land in somebody's cockpit—and then there'll be hell to pay.

There is another element of danger in swordfish—not to the angler, but to the boatman. I refer to the flexible cable leader. I know it is here to stay. I know that without it one's chances of landing a broadbill are slim. But that doesn't alter the fact that it is dangerous. With a big fish threshing and fighting alongside the boat, with fifteen feet of that sinuous cable whipping and looping, God help the boatman who happens to get an arm or hand caught in it. It is the most murderous device ever invented in the way of tackle. I think I am pretty nearly safe in saying that, if it had not been for the cable leader there wouldn't have been half the broadbill landed that have been. The reason for this is simple. The fish wraps himself up, gets badly fouled in it and can't get out. I have seen fish after fish badly mangled from the cable leader. Fortunately in marlin fishing it is not so necessary. A marlin doesn't roll as does a broadbill. Twelve or fifteen feet of heavy piano wire, with a swivel in the middle, is just as effective as a cable and not a tenth as dangerous. I haven't any patience with those who keep feeding line to a broadbill in the hope that he will wrap himself up in the leader and make his taking all the easier. If you aren't willing to go out there and whip them with your hands—if you can—don't fish for them!

A novice caught a two-hundred-fifty-pound marlin—a good fish. He had a terrible time with it for three hours and a half. Naturally he was very proud of his feat. Everyone was glad for him. Then there came a subtle change. Prosperity went to his head. That night in the locker room he reviewed the battle for about the tenth time. He grew eloquent when he told how it had taxed all his *skill* and strength. He deplored the fact that his boatman had been more a hindrance than a help. A couple of veteran rodmen had taken bad beatings that same day. Somewhat patronizingly he pointed out where they had erred and what *he* would have done if he had been in their place. The atmosphere got a little thick. At last Jump, who knew that man very well, cocked an eye at him and asked, innocently:

"How long do you say it took you to kill that fish?"

"Three hours and fifty-five minutes, Jim! And I want to tell you that I never let up on him a second!"

"Humph!" Jump grunted, and turned away. "You didn't *kill* that fish! He just *starved* to death!"

I frequently refer to "fish lanes," and mention the study of fish and their habits until a sort of sketchy jig-saw puzzle is formed. Perhaps it might be just as well to elaborate somewhat. I have found it a most interesting study. Perhaps you will, too.

First let us deal with the bluefin tuna of which so little is known. No one can say where they spawn, when, or what forces govern the cycle of their migrations. At times they appear in Southern California waters. Year after year they come back. Then, of a sudden, and for no apparent reason, they disappear. For years there is neither sight nor sign of them. Then, with equal suddenness, they come back. When they are not here, they are not reported anywhere else in the North Pacific. Where do they go—and why?

When they do come into our waters they are first reported in the vicinity of Guadalupe Island off the coast of Baja California. From there they can be followed to Forty Fathom Bank, which lies about halfway between the east end of San Clemente Island and Point Loma. Forty Fathom Bank appears to be a sort of rendezvous, a point of departure for their migration northward and westward. From there spread out seven great lanes of passage. These, if one knows one's charts, are as easily traceable as any of our major highway routes on land. Three lead up the coast, passing between the mainland and Santa Catalina Island; three between Catalina and San Clemente Islands; and one passes outside of San Clemente. This last, and outside lane, appears to be the one followed by the very large tuna. If there are others, they have not so far been discovered.

Along these lanes are banks, points where the ocean bottom thrusts upwards in the form of submarine peaks, plateaus and mountain ranges. Here the small fish, food for the big ones, gather, and here the big fish pause in their forward drive to feed and surface and loaf. And here it is that we find these big fish if they are in our waters at all—find them, that is, if we know our charts.

Between Catalina and Santa Barbara Islands the first six of the seven lanes more or less unite into one great artery which sweeps west and north into the lee of Anacapa, Santa Cruz and Santa Rosa Islands. These seem to form a barrier which turns the path of the migration outward on to Santa Rosa Flats a great forty-mile bank extending between Santa Rosa and San Nicolas Islands.

[219]

On Santa Rosa Flats the migratory fish, the tuna, albacore, marlin and broadbill, appear to remain for a considerable time. There they evidently build up their strength against the long traverse back to where they came from.

We have estimated that between Forty Fathom Bank and Santa Rosa Flats the rate of progress of the tuna is about three miles per day. But that is *only* an estimate.

Marlin follow, more or less, the tuna lanes, but with this difference. They seem to move on and off shore. By this I mean that one year they will be plentiful along the mainland and Catalina. Then in a year or two they will be scarce along the mainland, plentiful around Catalina, and moderately plentiful around San Clemente. Then a year or two later there will be none along the mainland side, only moderately plentiful around Catalina, and thick around Clemente. Then they will start moving inshore again.

Broadbill seem to fancy the lane passing nearest to the mainland, although they are found all the way out to Clemente and beyond.

Where do these fish come from? I wish I knew! As far as the bluefin tuna are concerned I have in my mind a great, lonely bank out in the Pacific, a thousand or fifteen hundred miles west of Cedros Island. For my own amusement I call it the Great Unknown Bank.

Marlin and broadbill come up from the south, probably from southern Mexican, or Central American waters. True, I have never heard of any of their young being found down there, but that may be because no one has ever really looked for them.

Now comes what to me is the most interesting and unexplainable phase of the migration of tuna, marlin and broadbill. I am positive that no one has ever *seen* or *taken* one of these fish that is on the back track home!

There are many, many factors which appear to enter into the movements of these migratory fish, but many of them seem at first glance to be so fantastic and far-fetched that I prefer not to set them down, despite the fact that I do think they have their bearing. As a matter of fact there is no thought of dogmatism in what I have written relating to the migration of fish. They are but my opinions and perhaps the opinions of a few others, based upon a good many years of observation. Quite possibly they are entirely wrong. However, the fact remains that they are sufficient for us and by reason of them we have been able to find and catch fish when others couldn't.

I once had the experience of fighting a fish of some kind for eleven hours without knowing then, or now, what I was hooked on to!

We were fishing for small tuna, twenty to thirty pounds. I had taken several and hooked another. I saw him strike and know that he was small. Halfway in something seized it and made off. I thought, of course, that it was a shark, but soon changed my mind.

Away it went in a heavy fast run. When it stopped I couldn't do a thing with it. I worked very hard, but I might have been tied to a rock for all the good it did me. For eleven hours I fought that fish and in all that time I *never gained an inch of line through my own efforts!* I could pick it up when we worked the boat over toward him, but he never let us get closer than seventy-five or a hundred feet. Three or four times we caught a glimpse of a big, brownish bulk in the water, but we could never make anything of it. At the end of eleven hours the reel froze and the line broke.

I wonder what it was? Since then I have been tied on to some big fish, but I never found one I couldn't move at some time or other.

VEILED HORIZONS

Now we have come to the end of this particular dead water slick. Beyond us the sea stretches away blue and inviting. The current has caught us and is whisking us onward. We have dipped a few odds and ends out of the slick—but only a few. Perhaps we may come across it again some time and pull out some we missed. Who knows?

ADIÓS